To David Maglaty

CITIES

from Nishita & Carter.

LAWRENCE HALPRIN

CITIES

THE MIT PRESS, CAMBRIDGE, MASSACHUSETTS, AND LONDON, ENGLAND

TO DARIA AND RANA
in a world at peace

First MIT Press revised paperback edition, April 1972.
Second printing, October 1973.
Third printing, July 1975.

Library of Congress Cataloging in Publication Data

Halprin, Lawrence.
  Cities.

  1. Cities and towns—Planning—U. S. 2. Urban beau-
tification—U. S. I. Title.
NA9052.H3 1972   711'.4'0973   70–39809
ISBN 0–262–08056–7
ISBN 0–262–58021–7 (pbk.)

It gives me great pleasure to acknowledge the assist-
ance of the people who have helped me with this
book. Adrian Wilson has worked with me continuously on the design of the book and I wish to thank
him, not only for his fine hand, but for his infectious
enthusiasm about its contents. Sue Yung Li, of my
office, has willingly moved from her drafting board
to the library and, with great dedication, has seen to
all the difficult technical problems of putting the
illustrations together, assisted by Tak Yamamoto.
And I owe a special debt of gratitude to my secretary,
Leslie Schenk, for her untiring patience, her ability
in working with me on the text, and for assuming
the many added burdens she has had to shoulder in
our office. I wish also to thank my associates, Landscape Architects Richard Vignolo, Satoru Nishita,
Jean Walton, and Gerald Rubin for allowing me the
time necessary to develop the ideas expressed here,
and particularly Donald Ray Carter; many of his fine
photographs have been used to illustrate our point
of view. Finally, I wish to point out my debt to my
wife, the dancer Ann Halprin, for many years of
stimulating exchanges of ideas on concepts about
movement and its relation to our total environment
as part of a long search for the meaning of art in our
society.

CONTENTS

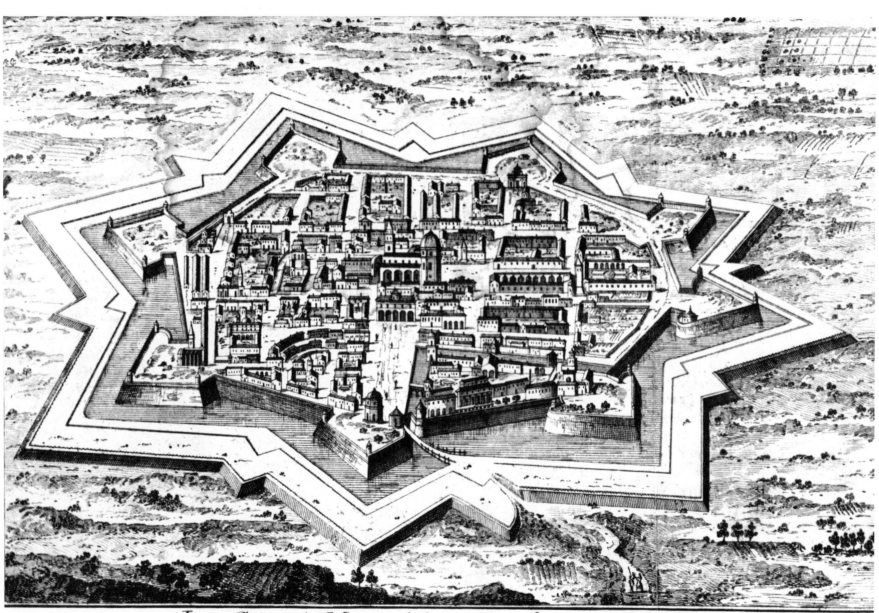

La Città di Mirandola nello Stato di Modena

PROLOGUE

This book is about the landscape of cities, which is to say, the open spaces, and what goes on in them. We will concentrate on the interstices of cities—as the matrix of urban life on the visual and physical qualities of the urban environment as a great form of art, and try to discover those elements which contribute to this environment.

The ultimate purpose of a city in our times is to provide a creative environment for people to live in. By creative, I mean a city which has great diversity and thus allows for freedom of choice; one which generates the maximum of interaction between people and their urban surroundings. In order to provide these conditions, one must start with the basic materials of urbanism. These basic materials and the way they can be structured are the subject of this book. Working with these materials, the urban designer must allow them to interact with the indigenous character of the city, its natural topography and views, its particularly unique features, its people and its cultural heritage. Only when these elements are creatively selected and processed can the resultant form of the city take shape.

We have no clear idea, I am sure, of the ideal form for a city. In other centuries at other times designers did have a clear picture of the form that cities should take. But their purposes in developing forms were perhaps clearer and simpler. The cities of the early Roman Empire started as army camps and were laid out on a strict gridiron to conform to a rule book, so that they would be easy to erect and to defend in hostile countries. Later the geometric form of many medieval cities, behind their walls, was governed by the need to repel invaders. Over the years, as each new military invention was discovered, existing walls were torn down and the forms of cities were changed to provide more adequate defenses

against the newer weapons (1). In Baroque times, the great avenues and round points at the apex of star-shaped avenues, radiating in all directions, were built for great parades and the control of their own hostile populations (3). They made it possible for a small garrison to take up positions and rake with fire and cross-fire any uprising of the city's own population.

But we are seeking an environment for creative living and the outward forms to achieve it are manifold. Though we do not have a clear picture of the ideal *form* of a city (4), we do have a clear image of the purpose of an ideal city. This purpose is clearly to make possible a rich and biologically satisfying life for all the city's people. What we are really searching for is a creative process, a constantly changing sequence where people are the generators, their creative activities are the aim, and the physical elements are the tools.

This book is an examination of some of these elements. It starts with the basic urban open spaces which give a city its character; the spaces within which its life takes place. First are the public open spaces: the streets, the plazas, the parks and then the private living spaces, the small gardens and private enclosures. These set the tone of the city, in fact, establish the qualities and the character of its presence. Then the more specific materials of the urban experience are considered, starting with the paving underfoot—the walking surface of the city. The discussion moves on to the vertical extension of the paving where flat surfaces shift in elevation into the third dimension and become steps and ramps and walls and the various barriers which are needed to prevent people from falling. Other chapters discuss other tools which can be used as basic biological ingredients in the city environment, such as water with all its many possibilities, the trees and

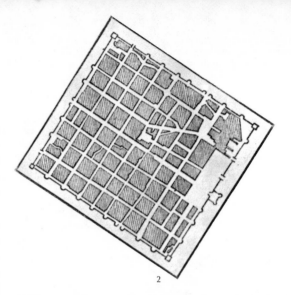

(2) The Roman city, Augustus Taurinorum, which developed into the city of Turin.

(3) Place de L'Etoile, Paris, with its radiating avenues.

growing things which we need to make our open spaces green and to maintain, even in cities, that contact with nature which we should have the opportunity to enjoy. We will touch on the furniture in the street, such as signs and symbols, sculpture and painting, and all those elements of micro-architecture, such as telephone booths and bus shelters which are needed to make the city street viable. As a result of putting some of these simple elements together, we start evolving the quality of a city, a character is established, a sort of physiognomy.

Finally the city comes alive through movement and its rhythmic structure. The elements are no longer merely inanimate. They play a vital role, they become modulators of activity and are seen in juxtaposition with other moving objects. Within the spaces, movement flows, the paving and ramps become platforms for action, the street furniture is used, the sculpture in the street is seen and enjoyed. And the whole city landscape comes alive through movement as a total environment for the creative process of living. We call this chapter the choreography of the city because of its implication of movement and participation—movement of people, of cars, of flying kites, of clouds and pigeons, and even the change of seasons.

We will not touch on many of the basic aspects of city planning which are fundamental to the functioning of cities and whose decisions are precursors to aesthetics. We will not attempt to cover land use or zoning, or economics, or the searing problems of mass transit and other important problems of group living, vital as they are. We are taking the next step after basic planning, where the planning organizes these necessities into an environment. The two attitudes are, in fact, one. For planners are beginning to realize, along with designers, that their function is to guide change; not to develop static form or fixed criteria, but evolving form. The search in our time is for valid processes, and our urban forms will evolve and change as part of our process of development and in response to the changing technological discoveries of the future.

In the search for valid processes, I have tried to avoid any implications of compositional principles, any rule book of urban aesthetics. These, I believe, tend to lead into a sterility whose examples are all around us—new squares with no life in or around them, enormous new buildings which look better without the clutter of people, beautiful old buildings torn down to be replaced by characterless new facades or signs in shopping centers all done in extremely *good* taste. These do not make a city. The creative city environment evolves as a result of both new and old buildings and a recognition that the city is a continuum, relating both to our past and our future. The provocative city results from many different kinds of interrelated activities where people have an opportunity to participate in elegant, carefully designed art and spontaneous, non-designed, elements juxtaposed into what might be called a folk idiom, a series of unplanned relationships—a mixture of what is considered beautiful and what is considered ugly. These relations are often subtle and even disturbing. It is an environment which should provide for those random and unforeseen opportunities, those chance occurrences and happenings which are so vital to be aware of—the strange and beautiful which no fixed, preconceived order can produce. A city is a complex series of events.

For this reason, I have used examples from all over the world and many different times, including some which are not carefully or even particularly tastefully designed, but all of which add to the colorful character and vitality of life in the city.

I remember with great clarity the greatest urban experience I have ever had. It was in Venice in winter. In front of the church of San Marco, the great square, which Napoleon called the most beautiful drawing room in Europe, was empty. It was cold and foggy and the top of the Campanile barely showed sunlit above the low hanging sea mist. The tide was in, and the black and white stones of the intricately laid pavement were covered with a thin film of water. There was no sound—no automobile exhausts, no buses. Absolute quiet in the very heart of a great city. In the distance you could hear faintly some young people singing. All of a sudden the air became dark with birds, the square filled with the beating of thousands of wings, the noise increased and increased until it was deafening, and the deserted square became absolutely filled with pigeons. The noise was incredible—even frightening. They had come to feed, and when they had finished, they left just as quickly, and the great square was empty and quiet again.

URBAN SPACES

The life of cities is of two kinds—one is public and social, extroverted and interrelated. It is the life of the streets and plazas, the great parks and civic spaces and the dense activity and excitement of the shopping areas. This life is mostly out in the open in the great urban spaces, where crowds gather and people participate in the exciting urban interrelationships which they seek as social human beings (5). It is the life of sidewalk cafes and museums and waterfront activities, of theatre-going and night clubs at night; the public city, bustling, active and exciting.

There is, too, a second kind of life in the city—private and introverted, the personal, individual, self-oriented life which seeks quiet and seclusion and privacy (6). This private life has need for open spaces of a different kind, which will be described in the next chapter. It needs enclosure and quiet, removal from crowds and a quality of calm and relaxation. The city should respond to both needs and both kinds of activity for they are equally important parts of the urban environment we are seeking.

Our urban open spaces are the matrix of this two-fold life. It is largely within them that we can find for ourselves these variegated experiences which make life in a city creative and stimulating. It is the open spaces which give a character and quality to our life in the city and establish its tempo and patterns. They occupy a position of central importance, if only because they usually occupy one quarter of the downtown area and often almost half.

Urban open spaces, of course, are of many different kinds and perform many different functions. In the most simplified and traditional form, they start as streets which provide access to buildings, light and air, carry utilities and cars and become, in fact, the very lungs and arteries of the community body. The main problems we are running into, in attempting

to keep our older cities functioning in our present, more complex society, is the multi-purpose use to which the old street has been put. It is being called upon to perform functions for which it was not designed. We need to specialize again and separate the functions which streets and open spaces are called upon to perform. It is too much to ask of a street that it serve, at the same time, for pedestrians and traffic and parking and shopping and children's play, and also provide amenity and quiet to the inhabitants along its way. Nor is it possible to expect a great civic plaza to serve as a storage space for automobiles, and a traffic circle, as a setting for a great civic fountain and civic pageants, and at the same time be a quiet, open breathing space in the dense fabric of buildings. Many of the great urban plazas in European cities are being desecrated and destroyed by making them into parking lots.

We need once again to evaluate our urban open spaces and to design them to perform ecologically for the good of the community. We must realize, too, that open spaces in a city are not decorative frills which can be added or subtracted at whim. Adequate open space is a hard biological necessity essential to life. We know, for example, the exact number of square feet per individual needed for other animals to live a normal existence. With chickens, give them two square feet or they will not produce eggs. And for dogs, 10 square feet per foot of shoulder height is necessary for them to live a normal, sexually adjusted life. Less than this makes them neurotic, sexually maladjusted personalities.

We do not know yet the exact ratios of open spaces which people need biologically for their lives and personalities to be fulfilled. But we do know of their importance, and of our need for constant contact with the elements of the natural environment.

6

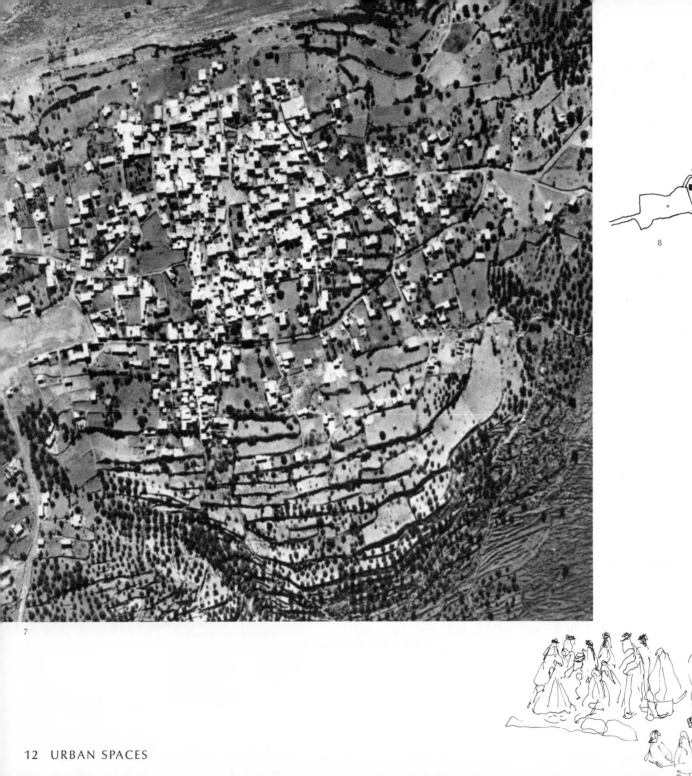

7

8

9

The picture opposite is of an ancient Arab city (7) set amongst terraces and groves of olives, in the hill country around Nablus. I have chosen it because it illustrates, in capsule, all the open spaces needed in a city. In this air view, the whole life of this small community is disclosed in clear form; when seen from this height its organic relationship of parts is immediately recognizable, and one can trace, as in a simplified diagram, the functions of its many open spaces. It contains a disposition of open spaces appropriate and necessary to every city and shows us in the simplest form the needs we must fulfill.

Approaching the city from the south, the traveler reaches first a large community open space, leveled and clear of any structures. It is in this space that community agricultural events have been carried out from time immemorial; it is a place for many people to gather and work together on the outskirts of the city, and it functions also as a formal entrance court, a community space for caravans of camels to stop and for merchants to set up temporary markets. This is the gate to the city (8a); it gives a real sense of arrival, a formality to this important event which the modern airport should at the very least attempt to recapture. One of the harrowing experiences faced by the daily American commuter is the dismal, visually offensive approach to the city.

From this entrance court two paths extend onward. (8b). The path to the east is merely a continuation of the approach road; it bypasses the city and leads on to more distant areas, so that travelers do not have to pass through the town unless they wish. It makes a clear differentiation in traffic flow and prevents the confusion between through traffic and local traffic so common in our times. These travelers who wish to enter this city take the westerly fork (8c); after entering they may go either directly to the center, or into the various winding streets which lead to the private clusters of houses. The residential streets are narrow, houses face onto them for access, but are turned inward to their own enclosed courtyards or groups of courtyards, where intense private outdoor living goes on (8d). The houses are intertwined and overlapping; some have their own private courtyards — small, open, roofless outdoor rooms paved with smooth stones for comfort; and some houses face onto community courts which serve a group of families. These neighborhood courtyards serve as outdoor living rooms, as places to cook and to hang the laundry; their stone floors cover great cisterns for the joint storage of water for use in the long dry season. They are active centers of family life. On the flat roofs, accessible from the courts, there are roof decks where, in the cool of the evenings, breezes blow and social hours can be held, and from which there are beautiful views of the city and the surrounding countryside.

If one follows the street system, one is led to the community plazas, several in number, which are scattered around the town so that every group of houses orients towards its own small community area (8e). One faces the school, another the administrative center, and the culmination is the great square facing the mosque and its muezzin tower, which forms the symbolic center of the city (8f). Adjoining the main square are the shopping streets and bazaar, the sidewalk coffee houses for games, for smoking water pipes, and for general male socializing. The plazas are irregular and many-sided, as in most ancient towns, with an unassuming, noninsistent quality of livability that makes them very pleasant to be in; though the bazaar is noisy and would not meet our modern rules of health, it is, as any traveler knows, exciting and colorful and pulsating with activity.

Every type of open space needed for the life of the community is here. There is only one type of space lacking, and that is a green park. But in a small city where open country is so close at hand, where anemones and cyclamen bloom under the olives only five minutes away from the furthest street, the city is *in* a park, and therefore, hardly needs one as a specialized area. This agricultural greenbelt, fixed by ancient custom, rings the city, providing open green space, limiting the growth of the city and providing a framework for its perceptible form.

Here, in an ancient prototype, are all those variegated types of open space which serve the many different kinds of human social needs. We need to capture, in our own modern terms, the simple, logical, and ecologically sound interrelationships which these ancient spaces perform so well.

(10) An ancient motel for camel drivers called a Chan, now used as apartment quarters by inhabitants of Acco, Israel. In ancient times the caravans stopped here close to the main square, tethered their camels in the ground floor stables and the drivers would bed down in the various rooms arrayed around the courtyard. It was a bustling, happy, exciting, adventurous place to stay, and the courtyard was used as a stage for all kinds of events. (It might be pointed out that camels are quiet beasts; their foot pads are soft and whisper as they walk, and they talk very little.)

10

Our own modern needs are, it is true, more complex than earlier ones. But are they so different? If we think of the new city as a complete environment for living, then it, too, will achieve the same simple, direct, biological qualities of its ancient prototype. The accompanying photograph shows a model of Waipio, a small city to be built in the near future in Hawaii (11). On a sloping site, the city is planned for a population of 60,000. It is a city designed for the automobile and bus—the types of vehicles which, in the forseeable future, will serve its inhabitants, though mass transport would be preferable. The overall pattern is urban at its core, which is to say, dense and concentrated. It has been formed to the strong sculpture of its surrounding hills and oriented to views. It contains a wide diversity of residential building types, including tall elevator apartments, in order to provide a wide variety of choice of living accommodations. Its road system is hierarchical. There is a clear differentiation, as carefully geared as possible to future traffic volumes, between roads bringing cars to the city, bypass roads, and the needs of internal traffic. In the determination of these roads, the most scientific system of computing traffic volume has been used. Houses do not face onto the roads, but inward to greenways and small private courtyard gardens for private living. The small residential street serves only for access to the houses on it; it does not carry through traffic and is safe for children and pedestrians, with underpasses under traffic bearing streets.

The types of open spaces are varied and serve different needs and functions. There is a broad ring of green open spaces separating this community from adjacent cities, serving as a greenbelt around it and confining its ultimate size. This greenbelt is used for hiking and horseback riding and close contact with nature. The major open park is used for more active games and sports, and includes a man-made lake for weekend boating, a golf course, and other recreational possibilities.

Pedestrian paths lead through greenways within the large residential blocks and serve as an internal circulation system for neighborhood contacts, children's bicycling, and walks to the city center. The paths vary in size between narrow ones for walking, widened places for sitting and socializing, and small internal neighborhood parklets. Eventually, they lead to the carefully located neighborhood schools, whose 7 acres of playgrounds serve each neighborhood.

The community focuses inward to its community center, centrally and symbolically located on a high promontory dominating the town. The center is a key to the design, for it establishes, at the heart of this new town, an intense and interwoven series of activities. It concentrates in one place all the diverse and complex interrelations of public urban life. At this center are shopping areas and restaurants, buildings for civic functions such as the library, museum, and post office, all arrayed and intermixed with hotels and elevator apartments, churches and the major community plazas in a dense and concentrated cacophony of mixed uses, where the life of the community will focus and establish its character. The automobile fits under the center, out of sight in underground parking garages which are linked to the plazas by handsome stairways. Within the center is a small green common area which is heavily treed and planted. Casual paths lead around a small lake at whose edges are grouped restaurants, shells for band concerts, and spaces for outdoor art festivals—a place for picnics and noontime lunches and for evening events. The malls and plazas around it are grouped into a series of outdoor rooms containing fountains, sitting areas, outdoor cafes and green garden areas. They are designed as a sequence of spaces with an eye to the people who will move through them, rather than as a series of formalized or picturesque architectural compositions. The framework they establish is one of possibilities, one in which it is hoped events can happen and the richest processes of life will be generated.

This new community has been started as a system of open spaces, each flowing into the other, each designed to relate to the life within the buildings surrounding them, and all together setting a firm ecological backbone for the growth and development of the community life of its inhabitants. It will be a long time before this community has reached its final form. The essential problem in establishing its design has been to find a kind of basic order to guide its growth, within which succeeding years and people can develop wide variegation and the sense of nonregimentation and unpredictability which creative life demands. The order has been derived from three firm elements. First and foremost is the way the community is adapted to its land and the configuration of its surroundings, the views and dominant topographic features. Next are the circulation system and the system of landscaped open spaces. These establish a pattern, a line of action, a framework for development. But equally important as this framework is the third element—the built-in possibilities for variation in growth, the attitude that constant and continuing attention to change and fluctuation is mandatory, and will depend on the creativity of the people who will be involved with it over the years.

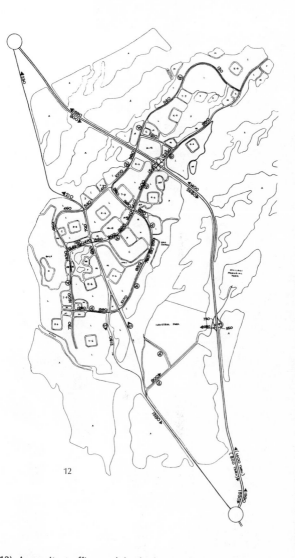

12

(12) A gravity traffic model which was developed for the new community, indicating volumes of traffic, origin and destination, number of vehicles, the critical intersection points and bus routes. Based on this traffic model, widths of streets and designs of cross sections were established, enabling a careful segregation between types of traffic and their integration with the total community pattern.

13

STREETS

The medieval street has intriguing characteristics for modern people. It tends to be narrow and winding, with an air of mystery and adventure. One does not see very far ahead, and the promise of fulfillment is always one step beyond. Houses line its course, tight up against the walking spaces, and the principal rooms face away from the street. The automobile here is an intruder, and, in fact, even today enters the street at its own risk. In early times, the street was a focus of neighborhood activity. It is still used for marketing and selling and the peddler moves up and down it crying out his wares. Here is the simplest multipurpose and vital part of the open space of the city, and even medieval Londoners understood the need to keep it clean and wholesome. A proclamation was issued to prevent housewives from throwing slop from the upper windows, or, at least, to call out a warning beforehand. We need to recapture in our own modern terms the aesthetic qualities of the ancient street—the quiet, the sense of neighborhood, the fine urban scale.

(13) A street in the Spanish city of Cordova. (14) The entrance to the bazaar in Nazareth, with drainage running down the middle of the street and shops along the side. (15) A street in Venice which has been widened to provide open space for a small market. It is not commonly realized that Venice is interlaced by streets in which the Venetians carry on the normal day-by-day functions of city living. Venice, centuries ago, established some of the principles of traffic separation we now realize are so important. The watery canals carry the traffic and service vehicles and the pedestrians and trees are on the ground. (16) A beautiful, long, curving street in Siena which surrounds the Piazza di Campo. Sequences of vistas of the Campo occur at rhythmic intervals (see Fig. 45).

14

15

16

(17, 18) Champs Elysees, a nineteenth century linear street driven straight through the heart of Paris by Baron Haussmann, Napoleon III's city planner. By its design the elegant, broad esplanade has separated the wheeled vehicle from the pedestrian. This early example of redevelopment in the city was executed without regard to the democratic process.

17

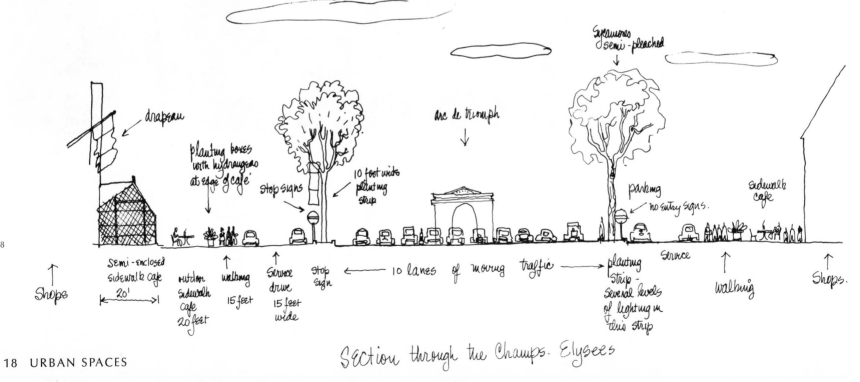

drapeau

planting boxes
with hydrangeas
at edge of café

stop signs

arc de triomph

Sycamores
semi-pleached

10 foot wide
planting
strip

parking

no entry signs.

Sidewalk
café

18

Shops

semi-enclosed
sidewalk cafe
|← 20' →|

outdoor
sidewalk
cafe
20 feet

walking
15 feet

service
drive
15 feet
wide

stop
sign

← 10 lanes of moving traffic →

planting
strip-
several levels
of lighting in
this strip

service

walking

Shops.

Section through the Champs-Elysees

(19) Market Street in San Francisco. An American version of the Beaux Arts linear street, it terminates in the Ferry Building tower. Remodeling is planned to separate pedestrians, wheeled vehicles, and local and inter-city traffic by multi-leveled structures. Open air arcades and widening of the sidewalks will give back to the pedestrians a shopping area free from automobiles, and bring light and air into the rapid transit stations.

21

22

In order to make possible a gracious, unhysterical kind of life on a city street, it has become clear that the automobile must take second place and be excluded. The next 5 pages show examples in various parts of the world where banishing the automobile has made life more enjoyable. (20) A street for little girls and hopscotch. (21) A street for gaiety. One of the pedestrian walks in the Tivoli Gardens, Copenhagen. (22) A street for shopping.

(23, 24) Sidewalk cafes in Venice—one of the most civilized and modern cities. One of the important functions of the street in Europe is the sidewalk cafe—a feature sadly lacking in America. (25) A new pedestrian bridge in Minneapolis which carries shoppers from one side of the street to the other over the automobiles. (Wanamakers did this at the turn of the century.) One would hope that the street itself eventually could be more handsome. (26) A pedestrian mall in the heart of Sacramento.

23

24

25

26

SHOPPING STREETS

28

The shopping street pulsates with excitement and an intense level of activity night and day. Here are great markets from all over the world.

(27) Hong Kong. (28) Taxco, Mexico—the most primitive type.

27

29

30

31

(29) The great Galleria in Milan. High, arching, and glass enclosed, it connects to the square in front of the Duomo.
(30) A typical cool, mysterious Persian bazaar whose appeal depends as much on smells and sounds as on visual qualities. As you walk through the bazaar, there are the tinkling of bells, the smells of spices, the smoke from waterpipes and the rich, deep colors of Oriental rugs.
(31) Galerie de la Reine, Brussels. Outside are the cars.

32

33

34

35

36

The new street for shopping is a bazaar made for our own times. Each one shown here has achieved dignity and amenity by the simple device of excluding the automobile. (32) A small square in front of Magazin du Nord in Copenhagen, an elegant place for shopping and sitting and passing the time of day. (33) The town center of the English New Town, Stevenage, and the hub of lively civic activity. (34) The famous Lijnbaan in Rotterdam, which rose like a phoenix from the ashes of the brutal, inhuman Nazi destruction. (35) A small alley in San Francisco, closed to traffic and connected to the main square. The beautiful archway to the right is the entrance to the V. C. Morris store designed by Frank Lloyd Wright. (36, 37) Two new shopping areas in America.

38

39

40

41

42

At the confluence of streets there are often small spaces which should be developed as handsome and colorful incidents in the heart of the city. A small plaza can contain, in a relatively casual way, sculpture, fountains, art exhibits, cafes, and benches which are human in scale, intimate, and usable. A local plaza gives a sense of place and becomes a focus for its neighborhood. It can be a rallying place for neighborhood activities and establish a quality and character for its inhabitants.

(38) The small Mechanics' Plaza in San Francisco, with its sculpture dedicated to the dignity of labor. (39) The plaza in front of the Comédie Française in Paris with its beautiful light standards. (40) A small plaza and arcade in Portofino, Italy. (41) A new, small neighborhood plaza in Sacramento, California. (42) The bustling Place du Tertre on the hill of Montmartre in Paris, a dense center of colorful activity, sidewalk cafes, and displays of painting.

MAJOR PLAZAS

The greatest major plazas in the world become civic symbols, not only because of their beauty of design, but because of the variegated and important civic events which take place in them.

(43) A plaza, Hebrew University, Jerusalem, the center of student life. (44) St. Peter's Square in Rome, with its beautiful colonnades by Bernini, is as much a symbol of Catholicism as the church itself, for it is here that hundreds of thousands of people congregate to listen to the Pope. (45) The Campo in Siena is not only the focus of governmental functions, but it continues to be the place where the famous horse races and festivals from medieval times are held. (46) The Piazza San Marco in Venice, that quintes-

43

44

45

sence of civic design, focuses within it the activities of outdoor eating, shopping, band concerts and religious festivals, to say nothing of feeding the pigeons. (47) San Francisco's Union Square in the core of the city has made the surrounding shopping area one of the most elegant and beautiful in America. Underground are the four levels of parking which make this feasible. The area would be improved if the streets surrounding the square were closed to vehicles and the garage were accessible by underground tunnels. (48, 49) New York's Rockefeller Center has become the focus of lively interest in the heart of a great city, not only because of its handsome design, but also because it accommodates a wide variety of activities.

49

46

47

48

NEIGHBORHOOD PARKS

In addition to the open spaces created by the major and minor squares which are usually heavily paved, there is need in the city for green threads and neighborhood parks which can bring the qualities of nature and a relation to growing things that we all need. Here, even in the city, children can play, birds can sing, and flowers can grow. (50) Tessin Park in the center of Stockholm, devoted to children's play, provides a green outlook for the surrounding apartments. (51) Bedford Square in the heart of London is heavily used by workers from the surrounding offices for lunchtime picnicking on the grass and strolling.

50

51

52

53

54

(52) A green recreation park in the center of a new living area in San Francisco. (53) Gramercy Park, a private community park, by its very existence, enhances the city and makes the neighborhood one of the most desirable in New York. (54) A green strip park along a canal in Berlin, by its simple presence and unassuming character, graces every neighborhood it passes in its winding course through the city.

CENTRAL PARKS

The major park in the city performs a weekend vacation function for city dwellers which is as important for their recreation and refreshment as the flight to the country. If we can maintain these great green areas and add new ones in the hearts of cities, they can help us maintain that ecological balance which our biology demands.

(55) Biology takes many forms. St. James Park in London is here shown as a setting for an important and universal need. (56) The incredible slopes of Central Park in the heart of New York City. (57) A quiet and leisurely appreciation of nature in Edinburgh. They are all waiting for tea.

55

56

57

(58) Golden Gate Park in San Francisco, a combination of activities of all kinds and for all people. This great park was created from a barren sand dune and its magnificent plantings, rollings lawns and riding and walking trails are host to as many as a million people on a sunny weekend.

59

60

WATERFRONTS

Most great cities have developed along waterfronts, which either thread through them as rivers or front on them as bays and oceans; they are the greatest resource for enjoyment and open space available to city dwellers.
(59) The French long ago learned how to use the Seine. It is urban, elegant, and readily available—a place for painters and lovers, stenographers, picnickers and fishermen. (60) A beautiful waterfront park in Stockholm. (61) A fine quayside along the Thames in London. (62) The colorful fish market in Copenhagen gracing its waterfront.

61

62

The American way with the waterfront has been much like our attitude toward all our national resources. There was so much of them that we did not value them highly. But now the time has come to recapture for ourselves those great opportunities which we have lost.

(63) In contrast to the beautiful treatment of waterfronts on the opposite page is the Embarcadero in San Francisco, typical of so many of our cities. Since the land was cheap and visual qualities were thought non-important, this has been the favorite spot to wedge in freeways and all the offal that comes in their wake. (64) The in-between solution, which is thought to be so gracious, along the Hudson in New York City is almost as bad. If you look carefully, there are five tiers of transportation facilities, including the original railroad right-of-way. It is true there are trees, but they are only decoration. The whole city has been divorced from the great Hudson River waterway by cars and railroad and freeway, even though the actual design is pleasant. (65) Directly across the island on the East River at the United Nations, is a handsome example of how these various elements can be designed in an integrated way. Through the simple device of building the freeway as part of the new complex, under the buildings and yet open to the river, and by building plazas and parks above, both visual and physical contact with the riverfront are obtained; the great activities of river boats moving up and down become part of the life of the city, and even the freeway retains its views and its amenity. Here the freeway has enhanced the city and given it a new dimension without destroying it.

63

64

65

GARDENS BETWEEN WALLS

I know of no great and beautiful city where people do not live close to the core. For the whole quality of a city's life—its personality and its image—is set by its inhabitants, not by its merchants or its tourists or the suburbanites who live on its fringes and scatter for home with the 4:30 whistle. It is the city's dwellers who fill its streets at night, use its parks and restaurants, populate its open spaces and plazas, and in the last analysis, fight for its amenities. When the city loses its inhabitants, it will die. And it will surely die as long as it does not provide a fine, well-rounded environment in which to live.

A vital part of this well-rounded environment in a city is daily contact with the out-of-doors. The simple pleasure of waking up in the morning to the sound of birds outside or the rustle of leaves in the trees is enough to help start the day joyfully. If you add to this the ability to step outside for a moment into an outdoor space, no matter how small, and get a glimpse of sky and a smell of damp earth and flowers, then the overwhelming scale and density of urban living can be largely overcome. And this simple biological amenity is by no means impossible to achieve.

Even in a large city, contact with the ground and life in a garden is possible. At extremely high densities, community gardens, jointly used by groups of families, may be necessary. Even these can provide adequately for outdoor family life, children's recreation, and a day-to-day contact with nature. They can be designed to form a central commons for surrounding houses and apartments. Or in the city, courtyard living is possible; rooms can face inward either to atriums or small private enclosures hidden by high walls for privacy. Each small space, if properly integrated into the fabric of living, can be designed to provide an outdoor experience no matter how simple.

It is necessary, of course, in these confined spaces, to shift our sense of scale and plan microcosmically. The tiny garden must establish its own scale—its own frame of reference—so that in entering it, one enters into a private world, into a man-made sense of isolation and remoteness. Through care in the selection of plants and textures, the careful manipulation of intimate views and perspectives, a quiet perception of out-of-doors can be established, even at small scale.

The Japanese, of course, have developed the small garden into a high art; trees are dwarfed, rocks are selected for their tiny perfect scale, and a whole natural universe is evoked in miniature. The Japanese garden is, in a sense, a series of symbols whose calligraphy is culturally understood through long accepted conventions. The garden for them has become an abstraction of nature.

Even without these symbols or these artificially dwarfed plants, nature can be brought into our city gardens, by pruning, by the selection of plants whose form and leaf and flower is in scale with the smallness of the spaces, and particularly by a careful reference to the indoor space of which the garden is an extension. Among the hard constructions of urban spaces, the confined and walled garden can generate a magnificent series of interrelations between man-made and natural forms seen at close range and intimately experienced—a complete universe in microcosm.

(66) A complete little universe—the purest statement of the private life in a city. (67) A small, recessed street garden in front of a brownstone in New York City. The hunger for natural forms expressed under most adverse conditions. (68) The residential street in a city can be made gracious by the simplest tree casting its shadow on a high wall. Behind the wall of this San Francisco residence is a private garden.

67

68

← 66

COMMON GARDENS

(69) A group of doctors' offices around a central common, all at ground floor level, Medical Plaza, Stanford, California. Each doctor's office has a small entrance courtyard which expands the use of his own office as a waiting room. The whole conception is that contact with the ground and a pleasant environment for patients makes the process of visiting the doctor an enjoyable one. (70) The enclosing fence surrounding the small garden of a pediatrician. (71, 72) Once inside the fence, the automobile is excluded and life can be idyllic indeed.

69

70

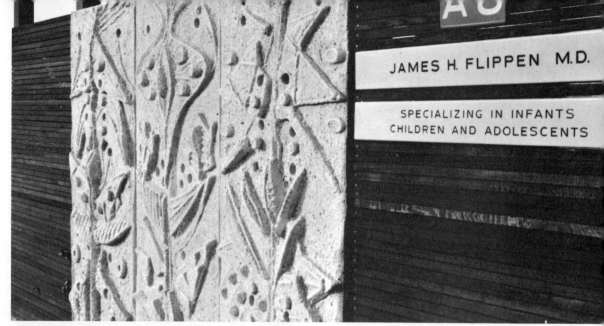

71

JAMES H. FLIPPEN M.D.

SPECIALIZING IN INFANTS
CHILDREN AND ADOLESCENTS

72

73

74

75

The combination of small private gardens joining hands with a central common makes possible a wide range of outdoor living. The private gardens adjoin the houses, and the centrally located common areas then can provide for more extensive children's play and outdoor community life.

(73, 74) This is beautifully illustrated in the heart of New York City at the backs of some old remodeled brownstones. (75, 76, 77) In a new development in Berkeley, California, called Greenwood Common, portions of each back garden were combined and allocated to the common area, which was built and is maintained by an association of the residents. Each private garden, though small, remains completely adequate for the demands of private living. On the facing page and on the next three pages, several of the private gardens adjoining the Common area are illustrated in detail. Each reflects the interests and needs of the persons for whom it was built.

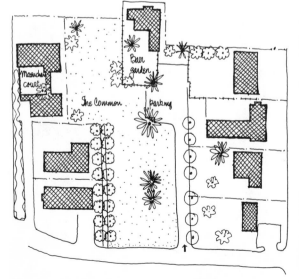

76

77

78

79

80

81

(78-83) The poetic Baer garden, which turns inward and yet maintains its relationship to Greenwood Common and to the great views of the San Francisco Bay to the west The owners delight in plants, and the intimate, small-scale qualities of leaf and flower and found objects.

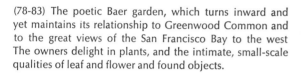

(84, 85) The Maenchen garden on the eastern side of Greenwood Common, completely introverted and built as a courtyard. The dimensions of the court are only 20' x 30' and all the rooms of the house open on to it.

84

(86) The Haas garden in San Francisco is wedged between the typical San Francisco wood frame house and the street. It is 13' wide and 80' long. Even in this narrow and confined space, the sun penetrates, the wind is blocked, and an outdoor life becomes possible. (87) The little Watson garden in San Francisco is a pocket edition of outdoor living, built around an old cherry tree which is great for climbing.

86

87

88

(88) Private enclosures in a city can serve many functions. Above is a small court in a new Parke-Davis warehouse, Menlo Park, California, designed by Minoru Yamasaki. The court provides light and air to the small office wing and is intensively used by employees for coffee breaks and lunches in good weather.

The four gardens opposite, from various parts of the world, show the quality of individuality which can be achieved in tiny outdoor urban spaces.
(89) A pot garden in Mexico. (90) A beautifully paved court-yard for a ceramicist in Denmark. (91) A small adventure alongside the Spanish Steps in Rome. (92) A surrealist garden for an unknown owner among the brick canyons of New York City.

89

90

91

92

93

(93, 94) The gardens for Manhattan House in New York City by Skidmore, Owings & Merrill. An excellent example of a varied and handsome way of urban living. The balconies for each apartment are enriched and enlarged by the common gardens on the ground floor which serve as a real and useful contact with the ground, for sitting in the sun, for pushing the baby carriage, and for games.

94

(95, 96) Allotment gardens in Berlin. The European tradition of urban gardens is different from that in America. For a modest sum, apartment dwellers can rent small allotment plots on the outskirts of the city where, on weekends or on balmy summer evenings, they can retire to grow their flowers and vegetables and sit in the shade of their own trees. The plots are small but intensively cultivated, and in addition to flowers, they also provide foodstuff for the table. The various small garden shelters are a vigorous form of folk art, and vary from small structures to elaborate expressions of the individual tenant's taste.

95

96

FURNISHING THE STREET

In the urban spaces between buildings is the paraphernalia of urban living—the furniture which makes these spaces inhabitable. Space itself is only an envelope within which events happen, and the city, like a stage set, demands modulators for people in motion—objects of use and comfort and artistry—guides for activity, shelters for incidental but necessary events, semibuildings, signs, symbols, places for sitting—a whole universe of objects. They are the small scaled elements which we constantly use and see; they set the dominant quality of streets and plazas, and by their ubiquity, they *become* the street. And like furniture in the house, they tend to proliferate, at times to whelp whole litters of new objects, which in aggregate can overwhelm the city by their sheer numbers.

Many portions of a city are, in effect, market places segmented into shops, stores or amusement areas; vying for attention, they display eyecatching signs to announce their merchandise. Starting with small announcements, the signs tend to get bigger and bigger, more and more raucous, more and more gaudy, until they at last destroy the very purpose for which they were designed. Main Street has become, in effect, a mass of competing signs, each more eyecatching and blatant than the next, a nervous, jittery conglomeration of visual chaos. If you add to this jumble the wires of overhead trolley buses, the scaleless brilliance of street lighting, the messy trash containers, the poles with traffic lights, directional signs, no-parking signals, mail boxes, fire hydrants, and other accoutrements of the Public Works Department, the street can in fact become a veritable dumpheap for necessary objects, ill designed, carelessly placed, and unpleasant. What architecture there is becomes obliterated, buildings are defaced and the street itself is a quagmire of confusion (97, 98).

The fact is that attention to the detail and design of objects in its streets is as important to the qualities of a city's aesthetics as its buildings themselves. There are, it is true, many necessary elements of street furniture which must occur at certain places and fulfill specific functional needs. Traffic lights, fire hydrants, directional signs and symbols, pedestrian guards, all need their definite places. But they can be well designed and related to the total scene on the street. More than these purely functioning objects, however, are needed in a city. Streets and urban plazas, parks and small squares, as has been pointed out, are the stages for city people's activities, and they need to be furnished with a whole range of well designed incidental objects for public enjoyment.

There are needs for benches and places to sit, handsome light fixtures with footcandle brilliances scaled to human pedestrian needs. Signs can form exciting collages related to the buildings to which they are affixed. They need not necessarily be pristine or sterile; in fact, they can sometimes even be gaudy. There is need for drinking fountains, bollards to control traffic, flags and moving signs, bicycle holders and small pavilions at outdoor cafes, newsstands and flower stalls. Not least of all, urban spaces should be re-established once again as the proper domain for the sculptor and painter in the city.

The modern city is a kaleidoscope of overlapping activities and people in motion. As the people eddy and move in a multifaceted series of actions, the furniture in the street becomes the fixed point which can guide and enrich their movements.

98

(99) A rendering of proposed remodeling of Market Street in San Francisco. The aim is to quiet the street down and organize the street elements into a dignified and handsome plaza.

99

(100) A major new plaza for the Student Union of the University of California at the heart of the city of Berkeley. The kiosk, light standards, fountains, flags and enriched pavings become the dominant elements in the open spaces.

100

LIGHT

Light is the medium through which most of us perceive and experience the world around us. But the qualities of light, of course, are non-static and constantly changing. Through seasonal, diurnal, and weather changes, the objects in a city are seen in different lights, in differing relationships, and in different degrees of clarity. Color itself, seen in shadow, is far more intense than seen in flat sunlight. Buildings acquire varying dimensions, weights, and silhouettes when viewed through oblique or horizontal light. Light imparts a mobile quality to even the most static objects.

But light can itself become a mobile, as it does in most cities at night. The great grey masses of buildings come alive at dusk with a blaze of multi-dimensional color; dull stretches of street become exciting and colorful, blazingly alive with pulsating rhythms of color. In the most brilliant examples, Times Square, Piccadilly Circus, the square in front of the Cathedral at Milan, whole sides of plazas become light mobiles. Buildings are nonexistent and, instead, we experience the most colorful overlappings of light collages on 100-foot high mobile canvases. How much more brilliant and exciting these could be if they were deliberately designed as part of the city's scene—changing, more mobile as a great light canvas in the heart of the city.

Light quality must be geared to specific uses as well. Many areas in quieter residential neighborhoods, at small squares and parks, need a warmer, simpler lighting geared to their own pace. Here the great, blinding glare of 1000-watt mercury vapor lamps, so uniformly and increasingly used throughout our city streets, must be replaced with lower-keyed incandescents, more attractive for ladies and more human in scale, closer spaced and lower. And each light, in turn, must be attractive to look at during the day when the pole, base, and transformer add a dimension to the street scene.

102

103

104

There are other techniques as well, some borrowed from the stage, in which light sources can be concealed and reflected from buildings and trees, others where small light sources hang in pinpoint effects from trees or arches of color. Blinking, moving, changing, they can generate a quality in the city environment which only amusement parks and gayways have, until now, been able to capture. (101) The main courtyard of the U.S. Science Pavilion at the World's Fair in Seattle by Minoru Yamasaki. (102) San Francisco at night. (103) Small pinpoints of light form an arcade in the Tivoli Gardens in Copenhagen. (104) The facade of a building studded with lights, Tivoli gardens.

105

106

Buildings used as light mobiles. (105, 106) Piccadilly Circus. The color scheme emphasizes the jolly English approach that any color is good as long as it is red. (107) The buildings opposite the cathedral in the main square at Milan.

107

(108, 109) Two views of the Milan Cathedral taken from the same position but at different times of day in different lights—early morning at cockcrow; late afternoon. (110) The beautifully sculptured light standards make an important statement in the Piazzetta of San Marco during the day as well as providing a soft glowing light at night. In the background are the two great emblems of the city on their pedestals facing San Giorgio Maggiore.

108

109

110

111

(111, 112) Two elegant cast iron 18th century light fixtures in Florence (above) and Copenhagen (right). The Florentine globe served as a prototype for the modern fixture shown at right, facing page.

112

113

114

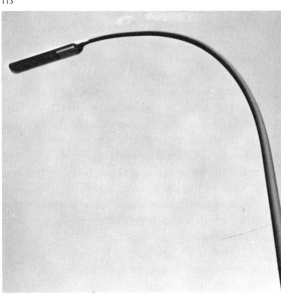

115

(113, 114, 116) Three modern fixtures designed for lighting pedestrian walkways in Old Orchard Shopping Center, Skokie, Illinois, Denis, California, and Spokane, Washington. They give a low level of illumination which is warm and human in scale. (115) One of the few well designed fixtures for high intensity light on highways. (117) Light standard, Sacramento, California.

116

BENCHES

Benches in a city are a focus of activity. For elderly gentlemen, they can be a place to sit in the sun and pass the time of day. They are places for students to study, for lovers to embrace, for young mothers to sit and enjoy watching their children playing, for shoppers to rest their weary feet. Elder statesmen have made the city bench a symbol of wisdom and thought. One can say that a city can be judged by its benches; their availability for use, their design, are a clear indication of a city's concern for its citizens' comfort.

There are two basic kinds of benches—one has a back, the other is flat and backless. The flat bench is adequate for short rest periods and simply enables the pedestrian to get off his feet. Flat benches tend to be more popular in architectural compositions, where they can be placed as sculptural elements in a plaza to imply amenity, without actually providing comfort for long periods of time. Thus they most often are made of hard masonry materials—concrete, stone, tiles—which relate more easily to the buildings which they surround and whose spaces they least confuse. They are also least susceptible to vandalism.

But the most usable and comfortable benches, the ones with the most flair and whimsy in design, are these elegant, backed benches which encourage the sitter to stay and spend some time in comfort in handsome urban surroundings.

There are endless and rich possibilities of design in the supporting members of benches, but very little variation in the actual proportions of the bench itself is acceptable (119). It should support the body properly by distributing body weight evenly over the surface of the seating area and, most importantly, incorporate an optimum seat-to-foot rest distance, so

(118) The quintessence of a bench, in Parque Maria Luisa, Seville.

that the feet can rest easily on the ground, the back of the sitter is comfortably supported and the danger of causing runs in nylon is minimized.

Finally there are those handsome, movable, iron chairs used so extensively throughout Paris in the parks, gardens, and plazas; and in the piazzas of Venice and Athens. These can be moved with the sun and the time of day and lend a mobile quality to sitting which more cities could provide for their citizens' enjoyment.

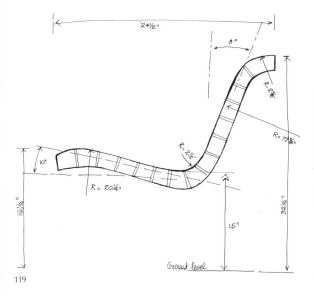

119

120

(120) A carefully proportioned double bench. Curvature and height have been calculated to conform to the most comfortable sitting posture. (This can also serve as a love seat.)

121

122

123

124

(121) A double bench in Florence. The supports are elegantly interlaced cast iron branches, and the seating surface is made of wood slats. (122) A Mexican tile bench, more picturesque than comfortable. (123) An ancient, encrusted incident in the Boboli Gardens in Italy. (124) A 19th century urbane cast iron bench in Mexico City.

125

126

127

(125) This example in Crawley, England, is unique, halfway between a bench and an outdoor chair. It has the great advantage of privacy, if that's what you want. (126) A wood bench incorporated into an elaborate series of planting boxes in Coventry. (127) The ubiquitous Paris double bench with a single back. A distinguished and straightforward statement of purpose. (128) The two elderly gentlemen are discussing important matters in an idyllic situation in Lucerne, Switzerland.

128

129

130

131

(129) Benches at the United States Pavilion at the Seattle World's Fair. Precast concrete relates in design and material to the structural walls of the building. (130) A wood bench on square iron legs serves as a resting place at the edge of a man-made lake in Spokane, Washington. (131) A wood bench cantilevered from a retaining wall on specially designed iron members. The wall is sloped and acts as a comfortable back.

POTS

On the hard, unyielding surfaces of city streets, plazas, and traffic intersections, flowers can grow in pots and containers; their bright splashes of color can do much to bring a quality of urbanized nature into the city. The city street is no place for grass or shrubbery or imitation rock gardens, whose captive suburban character can be worse than artificial plantings. But there is real place for plants in containers.

Pots have many advantages for the display of flowers or flowering plantings. They are readily moved; they can be easily filled with seasonal flowers which can be replaced when necessary, and they keep the flowers out of harm's way. When properly designed, they add sculptural elements to the floor surface, which even in winter, add much needed interest. There are many materials that can be used: cast stone, glazed or unglazed clay, wood, metal, cement asbestos mixtures, and fiberglass. The size and depths of pots should be geared to the plants to be planted in them. On the whole, containers are completely inappropriate for trees, unless they are large enough to support the trees adequately, which is very seldom possible. Even when it is achieved, much better growth will result when trees are planted directly in the ground.

Many cities, such as Stockholm, have carefully established programs for maintaining flowers in pots. This simply requires a vigilant watering schedule and three or four changes of flowers from spring through fall. Such programs add great liveliness and color to the urban scene and give a quality of change of season—a recognition, even in the city, of the great cyclical changes of nature.

132

(132) Precast concrete pots at the Washington Water Power Company, Spokane, Washington.

134

135

133

136

Here is a variety of pots made of different materials. (133) Bronze pots in the main square in Copenhagen. (134) Fired clay in Versailles; (135) The wonderful wicker plant containers which give privacy to the sidewalk cafes in Paris and are usually full of hydrangeas. (136) Shallow cast stone pots at the Science Pavilion at the Seattle World's Fair. Each pot contains a single color of tulip. (137) Nesting plant containers in a square in Rotterdam. The shapes allow for a wide variety of combinations and a massing of floral displays.

137

(138) A street of
pots in Sevilla,
Spain. The plants
are ivy geraniums.

138

139

SIGNS AND SYMBOLS

We have become oververbalized, and the earlier methods of visual communication unfortunately, are fast losing ground. We need to recapture them in the city—almost in self-defense—or we will become inundated with lettering and printed signs, each screaming for attention. Art in the street can bring with it easy communication. The early cigar store Indian, the bicycle hanging above the door, the barber pole turning and twisting its never ending moving peppermint stick, and the three golden balls which have signified money since medieval times were examples of well-known and easily identifiable symbols, indicating the business of the stores before which they stood.

In the clutter of our modern cities, there is a redundancy and an unnecessary length to the necessary informational messages which can be more simply and graphically presented. There are many things we need to be told about and informed of—pedestrian crossings, one-way streets, bicycle paths, no parking areas. Europe has already standardized many of these directional and informational signs into a handsome and simple system of graphic symbols.

In addition, there are vast areas of advertising signs which transform our city streets into a chaotic, endless, linear ugliness. The typical example is seen everywhere, a kind of urban nightmare not good enough to be surrealistically exciting, a folk art gone haywire, a hodgepodge of bad lettering, confused gigantism, disjointed agglomerations.

The opposite of this, of course, is the overpolite uniformity of signs in some of the newer, more elegant, shopping centers, where everything is carefully controlled, in good taste, and completely uninteresting. There is a point where good taste can become ineffably dull.

(139-157) The wonderful clutter of signs shown here and on page 70 is an early form of pop art, and has long been an inspiration to Dadaists. On the "strip" leading into many of our American cities, this form of folk art has gone stark, raving mad and turned buildings into derby hats or boots or hot dogs—a form of architecture called "Googie." But the quality of excitement, vitality, and direct appeal to the senses makes a vital contribution to our cities.

141

142

144

148 149

147

146

150

151

152

153

154

155

156

157

The city as a market place has always meant excitement, movement, kaleidoscopic color and sound. It is full of overlappings and strange juxtapositions. Much of this quality can be achieved through the use of colorful signs and symbols, mounted on buildings, hanging from canopies, painted on walls in the spirit of great collages. Attention to lettering and color, real concern for the quality of an entire street and one's neighbors, and a respect for the inherent shape of architecture (more than rigid design control) can give us both lively and well-designed signs in the street. An exciting environment of color, symbols, and letters—all thought of as painterly devices—can transform our advertising and communications into a great art form in the heart of the city.

(158) Some of the organized symbols which have immediate and direct meanings to all Europeans. They have been adopted internationally, and are seen on the highways and byways of all continental Europe. The triangular signs indicate danger; circular give definite instructions; rectangular are for information only. (159) The signs in action, in Siena. The ramp leading up through the archway has two signs above it, indicating no entry for trucks over 2½ tons. The arrow indicates the direction of traffic, rather than pointing to the important amenity below the ramp.

Danger Signs

DANGEROUS HILL | DANGEROUS CURVE (CURVES) | WATCH OUT FOR CHILDREN | ROAD NARROWS | BEWARE OF ANIMALS

Signs Giving Definite Instructions

NO OVERTAKING | TRAFFIC CIRCLE | NO LEFT (RIGHT) TURN | COMPULSORY CYCLE TRACK | NO ENTRY

Informative Signs

TELEPHONE | MECHANICAL HELP | FIRST AID STATION | FIRST AID STATION | FILLING STATION

158

159

161

160

(160) The ubiquitous and elegantly detailed Parisian kiosk, whose topknot shows its Turkish influence. (161) The Danish version in the main square in Copenhagen.

KIOSKS

Kiosk comes from the old Turkish word, "Kiusck," which means pavilion, and the term has crept into our architectural vernacular. We tend to think of kiosks as those handsome Parisian structures used to collect signs and notices of plays, movies and magazine articles into one organized space; these posters vie with each other on the kiosk in strength of design and color. They probably were the initial impetus for the development of collages as an art form, since the juxtaposition of the small, colorful placards was always quite random; the gentlemen whose job it was to glue them on simply found a vacant space, or overlapped an older out-of-date sign, and the resulting effect of differing ages and weathered qualities created a lively and colorful collage—like the European street itself.

But the city street must have other kiosks as well—incidental semiarchitecture which is needed to make a community function. Telephone booths, newsstands, candy vending areas, flower stands, bus shelters, ticket booths and, in parks, shelters for band concerts and picnics. Each performs its special function and takes its place in the city scene. These small structures can either clutter and uglify our streets or, through fanciful, even elegant design, add a note of gaiety and interest to our ordinary tasks.

(162) A charming example along the lakeside in Zurich. (163) A combination of bus stop and kiosk in a small plaza in Berkeley. (164) A small new metal kiosk in the main plaza at Capitol Towers, Sacramento. The under surface of the roof is painted yellow, and the supporting members are white, the panels blue.

162

163

164

165

166

167

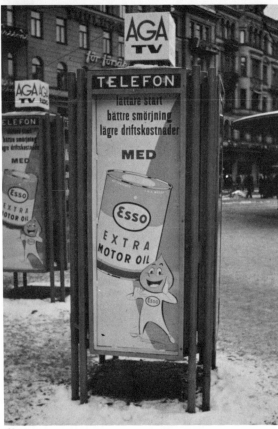

168

169

170

These are kiosks put to use—micro-architecture serving important functions in the city. (165) A bandstand in Mexico; (166) A bandstand in Sweden; (167, 168) Two telephone booths—one in Munich, the other in Stockholm.

(169) A place for children to buy confections in Tivoli; (170) Ticket booth for the monorail in Seattle. The roofs are moulded plastic; the colors are lavender; purple and red.

172

171

173

(171) The simplest form of bus shelter, in Amsterdam, whose roof and sides protect without overwhelming. (172) The famous Parisian pissoir. (173) A temporary canvas cover used as a band shelter for summer festivals in Amsterdam.

BICYCLES

First came the person walking in the street, and then he rode a donkey, a horse, or possibly, a camel. These older methods of riding through a city have given way in modern times to the bicycle. Halfway between the pedestrian and the motorist, bicycles give a mobility, an ease of negotiating traffic quickly, and an individuality and choice to motion which mass transportation cannot equal. Furthermore, it is inexpensive and easy. European cities, particularly, are jammed with bicycles; Amsterdam at the beginning and close of a day is a swirling, eddying mass of bicyclists in transit. More American cities, built on flat ground, could profit from the lesson of the bicycle. In New York City traffic jams, it is by far the easiest way of getting about. And doctors have made clear the value of the bicycle as a healthful method of exercising.

Like automobiles, bicycles require not only special pathways to travel, but parking areas for their storage, and here is their great virtue. While an automobile requires approximately 350 square feet for its existence (and at not less than $2000 per car for a garage, this can be expensive indeed), bicycles take up approximately 20 square feet; they demand less space and simpler, less costly facilities, to which a great deal of design thought and ingenuity has already been devoted.

175

(175) CIT porter relaxes between jobs in the Piazza dell' Esedra in Rome.

(174) Bicycle paths running along the highway in Belgium. These special paths prevent pedestrians from getting knocked down.

←174

176

177

178

179

180

181

(176-181) In areas where bicycles are a major form of transportation many ingenious devices have been developed for their storage. (182) Leidse Plein, Amsterdam, one of the city's busiest arteries.

183

184

185

DOORS AND ENTRANCES

Doors and entrances in the city have a great evocative quality which gives a hidden dimension to the street. They speak not only for themselves, of their own qualities as designs, but also of the life behind them—of hidden meanings, half-expressed relationships, of implied possibilities, even of secrets. A door can be an invitation or a rejection, an opening or a closing; it can invite the passerby in, or exclude him. In the past, doors have been objects on which sculptors and painters have lavished their greatest artistry, and they well deserve it. At human scale, related to the passerby on the city street with an air of great immediacy, they are the most personal aspects of architecture in the street.

(183) Door decorated for a festival in Mexico; (184) Sculptured door to the Baptistry in Pisa; (185) Door knocker and pull detail from church in Strasbourg; (186) An Art Nouveau shop front in Paris; (187) Entrance to the Herman Miller showroom on the old Barbary Coast in San Francisco; (188) A modern door in Venice by the American sculptress Claire Falkenstein. (189) A door to a walk-up apartment in Tacoma treated as a painting. The slot for mail and the doorknob have been used as part of the pattern.

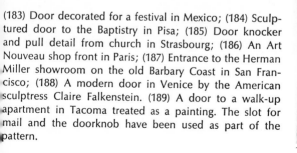

186

187

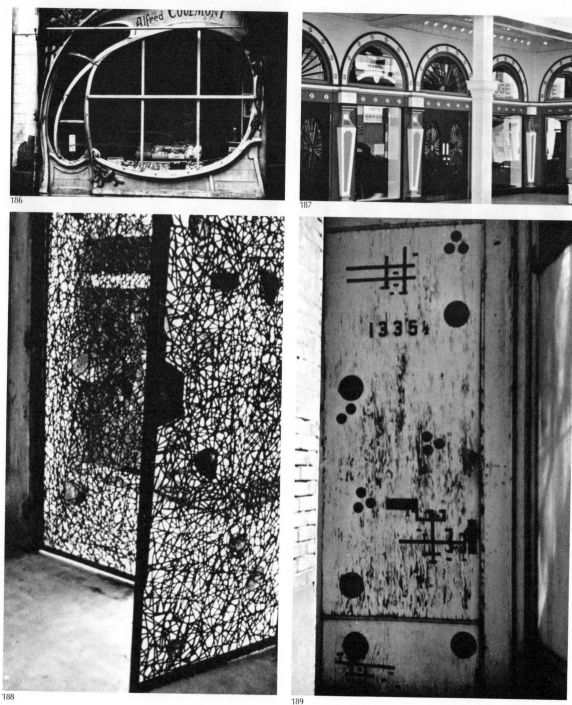

188

189

If the door speaks to the passerby, its hardware is even more immediately related to him as a person. These pieces of small-scale sculpture, in fact, are to *be* touched. Of the furniture in the street they are one of the elements with which one has immediate physical contact. Door handles and door pulls, bells, knockers, and push plates are elements which we grasp and touch, and which need to be designed as hand sculptures, whose pleasures go beyond the visual to the tactile.

Three transparent plate glass modern doors. In each, the quality of the door as a plane has been emphasized by the hardware. (190, 191) Bank entrance and doorknobs, Germany. (192) The entrance to a movie theatre, Venice. (193, 194, 195) Elements from a door in Florence. The complete door is shown on the facing page (198).

(196) The arcade along the Arno, Florence—a beautifully forced perspective. (197) Door to an artist's studio in Safed, Israel. Colors are green, red and violet superimposed on the traditional blue used to ward off the evil eye. (199) Art Nouveau entrance to the Paris Metro. An example has been placed in the collection of the Museum of Modern Art.

200

201

202

DRINKING FOUNTAINS

In ancient cities, the well in the square was a center of social life and gossip; in modern times the drinking fountain is not only a generous civic gesture but can be an esthetic experience as well.
(200) The Bernini fountain in the Piazza di Spagna in Rome;
(201) Water oozing from a rock in Spokane evokes a Biblical symbolism. (202, 204) Two modern fountains in Oakland and Berkeley use standard catalog fixtures in a fresh way. (203) A drinking fountain in a small square in Haifa, Israel, by Zvi Miller.

203

204

CLOCKS

An early form of mobile sculpture was the clock. Throughout Europe, on towers and churches, the hourly rhythm of the day was a signal for the most complex mechanical contrivances to activate moving figures. (207) Clock tower displayed at Greenfield Village, Michigan. (208) In our time, unfortunately, clocks have become less fanciful, but even in some of the modern examples, the works of the clock are displayed for the passerby as in this San Francisco scene. (205) Clock in the London air terminal. (206) The tower in the English New Town of Stevenage adorned by a modern clock.

(209) An elegant cast-iron street clock in downtown San Francisco.

205

206

207

208

209

210

211

212

213

(210, 211) The great Gabo sculpture in Rotterdam in front of the Beehive department store has become a symbol of the rebirth of Holland. When it was placed in position, there was dancing in the streets. (212) Near the Gabo sculp-ture is the screeching, searing figure by Zadkine—a symbol of the brutal Nazi bombing of Rotterdam. (213) Two metal sculptures in Paris. The one in the foreground moves and gyrates and is by Alexander Calder at the UNESCO Building.

SCULPTURE

Sculpture has always peopled our cities' squares with universal images of man's heroic idealized qualities. Sculpture should be seen outside; there it becomes an architectonic element more than decoration. It can symbolize all of man's aspirations; in fact, it can become so identified with a city that its image *is* the city. How can one think of Florence without its David in the Piazza Signoria or of Rome without its Marcus Aurelius placed on the Capitoline Hill by Michelangelo, and now of Harlow New Town without Moore's family group. Certainly, Rotterdam is Zadkine's tortured, bombed-out and twisted man, screaming against brutality but risen again as a symbol of defiance. These great sculptures are focal points which are vital elements in the hearts of cities; they are pivots in great plazas; spaces eddy around them, are pinned down by them, focus on them. Around them the life of a city moves and is made more meaningful. They are architectural echoes of an era made symbolic and should respond evocatively to the times. We need great sculpture in the street to comment on our civilization and speak of the condition of our culture, even, possibly, to throw stones at it. The meaning, today, of some of the heroic sculpture employing junk as its medium—old parts of industrial machines and automobiles—cannot go unnoticed.

214

(214) Carl Milles' people frozen in motion in his own garden, Stockholm. A man-made forest of vertical elements through which pedestrians can walk in a cadenza of art and living.

215

216

217

(215) The Barbara Hepworth sculpture is a focus in a new small plaza in Coventry. (216) Noguchi garden at the UNESCO Building in Paris, in which groupings of carved granite forms create an environment of sculpture. (217) The Museum of Modern Art garden in New York, which has become a meeting place in the heart of the city. There is no other outdoor space I know of in America where people can walk around amongst works of art as well as lunch and chat—it is a green oasis in the deep canyons of the city. (218) Brilliant and ephemeral junk sculpture in an assemblage built from driftwood cast up on the mud flats of the Bay at the entrance to San Francisco. (219) Detail of a wood sculpture assembled by Charles Ross from ancient bridge timbers.

219

218

CHILDREN'S SCULPTURE

Sculpture for children is designed for their participation and play, and one would hope to capture for everyone, including adults, the delight of these joyous sculptures. (220) The children's slide at Tivoli Gardens in Copenhagen.

221

222

224

223

(221) A maze-like combination of walls, paintings, slides, sculpture in the Tivoli Gardens in Copenhagen. (222) A cheerful monster in the Tivoli. (223) Two bears in the Lijnbaan, Rotterdam. (224) An environment of walled elements to play in; each is painted a brilliant color in a housing project for refugees in West Berlin.

225

THE FLOOR

The square of San Marco, like all the great urban spaces of the world, has beautiful pavings, elaborately designed, to make walking an aesthetic experience. The floor underfoot is a very immediate and personal kind of experience for pedestrians, but unfortunately, modern city builders have forgotten the visual and tactile qualities possible through the floor. It can be patterned, textured, colored, and thrown like a rich rug underfoot. In addition, the materials of floors strongly influence useability and comfort, as well as aesthetic qualities. The textures of pavings can guide the activities and movements of pedestrians, can even channel their direction, or prevent their encroaching on specific areas, or slow them down. Smooth materials encourage walking, rough surfaces inhibit walking, and though the ladies' high, spiked heel may not be with us forever, even flatter heels will slow down on rougher surfaces.

Traditional floor materials have varied, of course, with the regional availability of paving materials, although even in early times, paving stones were shipped long distances for special occasions. One of the primary reasons for the universal use of Belgian blocks was their utility as ballast in the bottoms of ships coming empty to the new world to pick up cargo. The simplest materials have always been native stones found in the area of the city. River-washed pebbles of different sizes and colors, set tightly together in rich and variegated patterns, have been a favorite for centuries. One of the earliest pavings used in great urban plazas was split or quarried flat stone. These were normally cut in square shapes and laid in many different patterns and combinations of colors. The Capitoline Square by Michelangelo uses cut travertine with a field of small basaltic blocks. There are many other paving blocks which can be set by hand as well; cobbles, granite setts,

(225) Round river stones, brought up from the local river bed and dumped at random on the floor of the street, form the simplest paving, as in this city in Spain. Stones control the mud but are inadequate for wheeled vehicles, and difficult even for donkeys to negotiate.

OF THE CITY

tiles, different kinds and colors of marble, from the soft, pitted travertines to the hard, veined ones, and many clay materials fired in hot kilns to harden, such as brick, baked clay, adobe and coal. Wood block sections cut from trees and even the bones of whales have been used to pave our city streets.

The great advances in modern paving have been made in the use of materials which are poured in liquid form and harden in place, and these can cover great areas quickly and easily and, therefore, cheaply. Elaborate mechanical devices have been developed to mass-produce the method of pouring. These poured pavings include concrete and the various asphalts, terrazzos, and stabilized earths, and each can be used to cover large areas quickly and efficiently. Today, the small hand set paving block is an expensive luxury in most industrialized countries, and except under conditions where labor is cheap or for special reasons (such as the constant sinking and need for resetting in Holland), is not widely used. In spite of cost, however, they still have uses, even practical ones, such as in situations where underground utilities may have to be reached frequently. But their most common modern use is for their pattern, and the small, handcrafted, enriched quality which they can bring to the walking experience. The search today is for methods, in our industrialized civilization, of texturing and coloring the relatively inexpensive poured materials and of combining them with the hand set pavers for enrichment. And there is a great deal that can be done. Concrete has endless potential—its surface lends itself to great variations in finish—from very smooth to rough; even washed off with water while still soft to expose the pebbles which form its matrix. It can be colored as well as textured, scaled to human measure by the use of regular insets of other materials; scored and patterned with simple or specially made tools—even painted.

Asphalt, too, though less subject to various textural and color treatments, is a handsome and variable poured material. The major problem in its use as a pavement in the city is its softness when it is not under the constant kneading action of automobile traffic. Under the impact of the 2000 pounds per square inch force of the modern spiked heel, it simply does not hold up. And it does not lend itself to quite the number and variety of surface textures as does concrete, although the surface material and quality does allow some variation in color and texture. Its very drawbacks are, of course, also its advantages; for the soft qualities of asphalt give it a resilience and a slight spring which makes walking on it a pleasant kinesthetic experience.

226

(226) Pompeiian stones are used in a more organized fashion; there is a very clear functional separation between the needs of wheeled vehicles and pedestrians. The roadbed carries the chariots; the raised stepping stones allow pedestrians to cross at street corners and are spaced to permit chariot wheels to pass between them. The curbing stones define the edge of the pavement and protect the pedestrian from the chariot wheels.

(227) A medieval pavement in the old ghetto of Mea Shearim in Jerusalem. The local stone has been quarried and cut and laid in a simple running bond pattern, with a crown in the middle of the street to carry drainage to each side.

227

GRANITE SETTS

(228) For centuries, the favorite common paving in the streets of Europe has been granite setts. These are quarried in a 4" x 4" x 4" dimension and laid in sand on a carefully tapered hard base course. The Champs Elysees in Paris is shown being repaved with these blocks, which were used to make barricades during the war.

229

230

(229, 230) The pavers are brought in and dumped in a windrow, and the workers set the paving in a fan pattern—in a circular movement, as wheat is cut with a scythe. The pattern is easy to lay and provides a very stable paving because of the wedging of each stone and its nonalignment with the direction of traffic.

231

(231) The fan pattern of paving is used extensively, not only as a road paving, but also as a handsome and maintenance-free floor for many of the major plazas of Europe, as in de Dam, Amsterdam.

232

(232) Paved plaza in front of the memorial to the Russian dead, Treptow Park in East Berlin. Urban squares and streets which are heavily used by pedestrians need a walking surface with some of the qualities which, in nature, would be evoked by grass or wildflowers in the woods. This quality underfoot can be man-made by laying small cut stones in diverse and complicated patterns. The cost, of course, is high in industrialized countries, but in areas where unskilled labor is available, this kind of paving is still used.

(233) The UNESCO garden paving in Paris by Isamu Noguchi. (234) Paving in Copenhagen by Langkilde. (235) One
of the most beautiful modern floors in Europe, the main
plaza of the New Town of Vallingby outside Stockholm.

233

234

235

236

PEBBLES

(236) In the urban environment it is a pleasant thing to combine natural forms with hard constructed forms, and this is achieved by the use of stones of various sizes in combination with plants. At Harlow New Town existing trees were saved in a small plaza, and the raised mounds, used as sculptured elements, maintain the original ground level of the trees. The mounds are covered with stone setts, which replace planted ground covers, and small stones give much the same fine-grained texture as grass lawn.

(237) A combination of plant material and stones in Harlow. Each enhances the other, and the contrast between the two is one of material rather than texture.

237

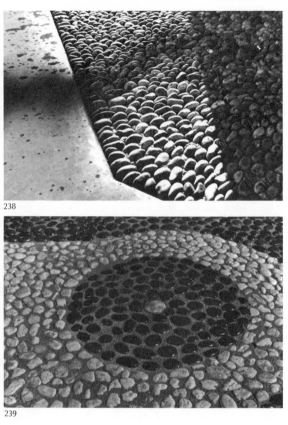

238

239

Pebbles can be laid either flat or on edge. In former times they were bedded in clay, but nowadays they are laid in a topping course of rich cement poured over a 3″ roughly poured concrete base. (238) If they are laid on edge, the pebbles extend above the base and will dominate; the concrete will hardly be visible. These are most appropriate for areas where walking is to be discouraged, since the spaces between the pebbles make them difficult to negotiate. (239, 240) If walking is to be encouraged and the pebbles are simply for pattern, they should be laid flat. Their surfaces will then be level with the concrete matrix because the rounded edges of the pebbles touch below the surface and force the concrete up between the stones.

240

COBBLES

Belgian blocks called cobbles paved most of the streets of Europe, and they were always a favorite with revolutionaries. The blocks were easily ripped up and made into barricades or thrown at soldiers; their 12" x 4" x 8" dimensions made them excellent weapons. They were the usual road surfacing material in early years of the new world, but the noisy clatter of metal-clad wheels and the bounce of tires have caused most city engineers to cover them with asphalt in modern times, which is a shame.
(241) At the edge of a small canal in Strasbourg. (242) Sidewalk in New York along Central Park.

241

242

CUT STONES

The great virtue of flagstones for paving is the intricate and chance patterns they establish—impossible with any more modular material. There are two ways in which they can be laid.

(243, 244, 245) Careful dressing and selection of stones are needed to lay a closely jointed and fitted paving used in Jerusalem. (246) Paving on the Island of Mykonos, where the stones are laid as they come from the quarry and the spaces are chinked with smaller stones. The stones are outlined with lime to emphasize the pattern; the frequent whitewashing helps to keep the valuable rainwater clean on its way to the deep underground storage cisterns.

243

244

245

246

247

248

Cut stones make intricate and beautiful patterns appropriate for urban squares. (249) The famous knot-like pattern at San Marco is a combination of white travertine and a black basalt. (247) In the piazza at Milan the use of stone is most elaborate, combining square and rectangular cuts with fields of a randomized ashlar. (248) In a modern example in Detroit, Minoru Yamasaki has fitted together an intricate and beautiful repetitive pattern of triangular shapes.

249

(250) A detail from the new path leading up to the Acropolis in Athens. This beautiful and rhythmic pattern has been achieved by using old stones laid in a long, flowing sequence almost like a musical score for jazz. (251) A modern example in Fort Worth designed by the author. A dominant gridded scheme is fragmented by random pieces of many sizes, creating a painterly collage-like pattern. (252, 253) Enormous blocks of stone establish a strong, large-scale quality to the streets in New York and Milan.

250

251

252

253

BRICK

Brick is a symbol of slavery, and so it is strange that it has become such a favorite and human sort of paving in our times. It was while watching a Hebrew slave mix straw and clay for the brick kiln in Egypt that Moses slew his first overseer. Besides the innumerable number of patterns in which it can be used, there are wide gradations in the color and texture of brick surfaces. The two most common textures depend on the method of moulding. The sand mould

255

256

brick has a smooth finish, and the wire cut a rougher, more porous surface. Both come in several dimensions—the usual is 2⅜″ x 3¾″ x 8″, the Norman is 2¼″ x 3¾″ x 12″, and the Roman is 1⅝″ x 3¾″ x 12″. The important point in selecting paving brick is that it be high-fired, hard surfaced and resistant to wear and cracking. (254, 255, 256) The basic patterns are running bond, herringbone, and basket weave.

259

257

258

(257) Brick lends itself to widening of pavings without the difficulty of matching patterns—such as in the restoration work at Williamsburg. (258) A modern example, in which a precast insert of concrete sits in a field of brick. (259) At Old Orchard Shopping Center outside Chicago, the brick is laid as a colorful rug in the center of a plaza.

260

261

262

263

264

265

The most widely used modern walking surface is concrete. It is inexpensive and easily poured, and, if expansion joints are installed adequately and proper attention is paid to re-inforcing, it can last for centuries without serious cracking. (260) The surface treatment possibilities are almost un-limited, and they depend in large measure on the final method of troweling by the concrete finisher. (261) A steel troweled, simply scored, example. (262) A method of scor-ing with specially designed tools. (263) Crude but crafts-manlike striations to prevent slipping on a ramp. (264) The sidewalk has first been smoothly troweled, and then finally brushed with a stable broom in one direction, with an area on both sides of the scoring lines left smooth to create a simple, grid pattern. (265) The almost irresistible quality of a newly poured paving demands the best from the artist.

CONCRETE

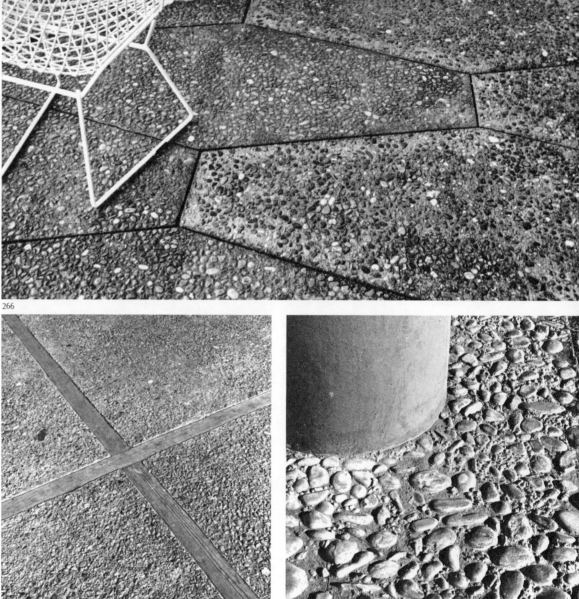

266

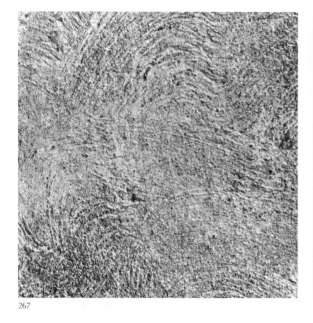

267

268

269

(266) Concrete with a seeded surface. After the rough pour, carefully selected small river stones have been dumped on the surface, tamped in, and then the surface film of cement carefully washed off. (267) A sweat finish. This is a simple, handsome method of roughening the surface by pulling the wet concrete slightly in a rotary motion with a wooden trowel. (268) Exposed aggregate, widely used in California. It has also been called frozen gravel or pebbled concrete. The concrete is poured between wood grids and after four or five hours of hardening, the surface is washed with a fine stream of water to expose the pebbles used in the concrete mix. (269) This is accomplished in the same manner as the pebbled concrete, but with the use of a heavier stone aggregate.

270

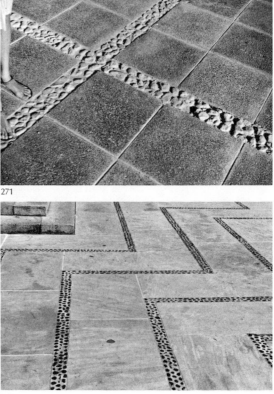

271

272

Vast areas of paving in large, heavily used plazas can be brought into human scale by enriched expansion joints and modular grids, which can be in as many combinations of materials as invention allows.

(270) The main plaza of the Berkeley Student Union, where the field is exposed aggregate and the grids are running bonded brick. (271) Detail of the main plaza of the Hebrew University in Jerusalem. A combination of precast concrete paving blocks and a stone grid. (272) Black Mexican beach pebbles set in a linear calligraphy between stone pavers.

PRECAST PAVERS

Precast concrete paving units allow a much closer and uniform control of surface textures than concrete poured in place. Their cost is halfway between stone and poured concretes, and they are particularly useful in areas where settlement of the base is a concern. If settlement occurs, units can be reset; this also applies where segments of paving may have to be lifted out because of underground utilities. (273) The town square at Stevenage is paved with precast units in combination with Belgian blocks.

ASPHALT

274

275

276

Asphalt is the symbol of all that is worst in the city, and the asphalt jungle has become a synonym for an unpleasant environment.

(274) Certainly the Berkeley school yard shown here illustrates why. It is inhuman, lacking in scale, and prisonlike in its quality; one is sad because the children are imprisoned there. But this is not the fault of the material, but rather in the way it is used. (275) Children's drawings in a playground show the creative uses to which asphalt can be put. (276) In the square in front of the Parliament in Athens, the beautiful plaza has been paved in asphalt with a white travertine grid.

277

278

279

280

In asphalt as well as concrete, precast hexagonal units are available and are widely used for paths and park paving. The scale of the unit is fine and the wearing surface is soft enough to give a slight resilience to walking.
(277, 278) Fifth Avenue, New York. Asphalt used with cobble can result in a combination of very handsome colors. (279) Here the brick was laid first and then the asphalt hand tamped in the interstices to make a transition between the two materials. (280) Asphalt textures can be as handsome as exposed aggregate, depending on the grades of asphalt and the size of the stones used in the mixture. This surface texture can be most variable, depending not only on the mix but on the seal coat which is used and the amount of wear that the surface receives.

281

282

283

284

MISCELLANY

In addition to the more common types of paving, there are innumerable others which make use of locally available native materials. (281) Whalebone squares in front of the courthouse of the City of Monterey, which was the headquarters of the whaling industry in California. These 8" sections are cut out of the spinal columns of whales and rammed into the mud sub-base. They have been in place now for about 100 years and have every indication of surviving until whaling comes back again. (282) The wood blocks in the front courtyard at Versailles. Wood has always been used throughout the world as paving. In California, redwood blocks or cut sections of railroad ties have been used for many years, and there are still wood block pavings in the streets of Chicago. When pressure-treated with creosote or other preservatives, it is a very longlasting material, if only the heart wood of the tree is used. (283) Small glass block inserts bring light into underground basements. (284) Terrazzo, one of the most common urban pavings used today, is slick, slippery and unsympathetic underfoot.

285

The floor is full of holes which lead to underground mazes of vast complexity and enormous significance to a city. Underground are the sewers, subways, basements, and gas and electricity lines which make a city function; the holes in the floor are portals through which they are reached. (285) The inserts are usually made of cast iron, which can become part of the floor pattern, as in the beautiful paving of the Milan Galleria. (286) An elegant cast-iron manhole cover in El Greco's garden in Toledo.

286

DRAINS

The floor is dimpled with catchbasins; they are the drainage beginnings of a long, watery trek to the sea. In great plazas, they occur frequently enough to become a significant part of the pattern of the floor. (287, 288) In the Campo in Siena the whole plaza is focused toward the great drainage orifice at its apex.

287

288

289

290

291

292

293

(289-292) These examples of catchbasins are from cities in Europe; many of the metal ones have a swirling, moving design which expresses the motion of the water sieved through them. (293) An American example of a standard factory-made grating, inserted into a stone mosaic water-course.

294

(294) Burning incense on the steps of a church in Chichicastenango, Guatemala. These steps are a focus and center of civic activity.

THE THIRD

As the floor of the city changes levels, the walking experience achieves a new quality and a different dimension. Through steps and ramps, platforms and long sloping planes, the horizontality of plazas and squares acquires a new sense of drama. By emphasizing these variations even the most mundane and everyday occurrences can achieve grandeur and assume the evocative qualities of dance and theatre.

Many changes in elevation are functionally necessary, particularly in cities built on hills. Mounting a hill from one level to another and the gentle climb along the gradually sloping street, running with the contours, are physical necessities in hilly country. These requirements can either be difficult and annoying chores despite the need for physical exertion, or fine kinesthetic experiences, depending entirely on how they are designed.

Many of the great staircases in the world have transformed a necessity into an artistic experience. The beautifully articulated qualities of the Spanish Steps in Rome, with their rhythmic variations broken up by level platforms, and their continuing curvilinear, flowing lines are a great theatre piece in the heart of the city. They function in the most unexpected ways as a stage set for continuous and varying activity, which ebbs and flows with the time of day, the weather and the moods of the Roman people. Beyond the sheer qualities of vertical movement which they generate, these steps, in addition, become staging areas for activity. They are favorite platforms for meetings, for discussions, for children's play, for young men to ogle girls, for flower selling— the center of the most complex order of events.

Since the most ancient times steps have been used to dramatize events; they have always been places to make speeches and harangue crowds. In medieval times, they were the only stages; it was on steps that

DIMENSION

the great Passion plays were acted out under the shadow of the church and viewed from the plaza; their elevation gave emphasis and dignity to these events. Steps have been places for beggars and preachers, money lenders and prophets; podiums for the unusual.

There are other ways of accommodating vertical motion in a city. Where steps are inappropriate because of the passage of wheeled vehicles or there is more room to accommodate variation in elevation, ramps can be used; these establish a different quality of movement—more fluid, even more intense. One can pause to rest on a flight of steps, stand, sit down. But on a ramp there is the continuous downhill pull of gravity; the effort needed to push against gravity when moving uphill makes walking on ramps a continuous flowing experience, not a staccato interrupted one. Ramps must be carefully proportioned or they become dangerous and non-negotiable. The most comfortable ramp for walking is one in which the rise is 1 foot in 20 horizontal feet. This generates a gentle and comfortable feeling of walking uphill or floating downhill with a minimum quality of conscious effort. The calculation of the amount of force needed to negotiate ramps of different slopes becomes a fascinating tool for the designer. Through the use of ramps, the walker can sense in his own body the qualities of the city environment through his own physical involvement.

In addition to the shifts in the floor planes, the third dimension in a city is dominated by the vertical walls of houses and buildings and the other architectural constructions which define the spaces and line the streets and plazas. Here the matter of human scale becomes of paramount significance. We can crane our necks at the great height of skyscrapers and tall buildings and goggle at the enormous scale and magnificence of urban constructions but the intimate quality of a city is achieved by those things which we experience in the 20 or 30 feet from floor level within our normal line of sight. These are the vertical architectural elements to which we can relate at our own personal and human scale. In this range are the walls and railings, the barriers and impediments to motion, the urban artifacts which modulate our activity—all the small scale elements which give a personal impact to architecture and its environment. At this level the textured walls become an immediate experience, the bollards and railings which channel pedestrian movements are physical barriers which we can touch and feel, and the important tactile qualities of the architecture set the tone of the city.

If these small scale elements of architecture are given proper emphasis, then buildings can reach any conceivable height without loss to human scale.

295

(295) This great staircase in Macao leads to the facade of a church now long since gone, but its drama and sense of uplift still remain. (296) The bottom of the Spanish Steps in Rome which serve as a young people's club.

296

297

STEPS

Steps at the base of a building give a sense of dignity and serve as a transition to the ground on which monumental structures stand.

(297) The Duomo in Orvieto, with its bi-colored marble striping, is carried down into the ground in color and levels by the broad steps at its base. (298) At the base of the Baptistry in Pisa, where the steps form a series of benches for al fresco lunches. (299) The broad steps leading down to a fountain and pool at the Hadassah Medical Center, Jerusalem, emphasize the drama of the water in its setting and serve as platforms from which to view the watery effects. In the background is the small synagogue in which the Chagall windows have recently been installed.

298

299

(300, 301) The Spanish Steps leap up the great hill from the Piazza di Spagna in a series of rhythmical variations akin to the experience of a dance sequence. (302) The broad, shallow steps leading from the street down to the main plaza in front of the Crown-Zellerbach building by Skidmore, Owings & Merrill. Each tread has a different dimension.

300

301

302

Slight variations in elevation can be used to emphasize and dramatize the shifting planes of a plaza and bring a quality of dimension to the flat surfaces.

(303) A small sunken plaza in Lincoln, Nebraska. (304) Orvieto steps. The riser has been sculptured with the name and crest of the donor. (305) Three steps in Palo Alto, California insert their curved calligraphy between two flat planes.

303

304

305

306

307

Steps shift into platforms, and in the process, achieve a theatricality and a sense of drama.
(306) Private ghats, near Wai, India. (307) Plaza, Amsterdam.

308

Steps can be built to get people quickly from one level to another without concern for physical comfort.
(308) The ancient Crusaders' steps, Israel, were simply a way for archers to mount the battlements quickly on a run. They are beautiful but very difficult to climb.

(309) An ancient stepped street in Assisi, between stone-walled houses, which, by gentle curves and slight offsets, makes the adventure of walking from one level to another a visual delight. (310) At the Port Authority Bus Terminal in New York City great numbers of people are moved easily and rapidly, but this escalator lacks the aesthetic qualities which are so important a part of the ancient medieval city. (311) A spiral fire escape, UNESCO Building, Paris. Under normal circumstances, it would be difficult to negotiate, but it has been designed primarily as a freestanding piece of sculpture whose spiral form contrasts with the recti-linear modules of the building.

309   310   311

312

313

314

The city street in hilly country can become so steep as to make sloping sidewalks slippery in the rain and dangerous for walking. The combination of steps and ramps solves this problem and allows two different types of movement.

(312, 313) San Francisco. (314) A combination of ramps and steps in Italy. The risers are travertine, and the treads are of Roman brick laid in a herringbone pattern.

RAMPS

(315) Ramps on the south bank of the Thames in London overlooking Big Ben undulate the surface of the plaza, giving it the qualities of a stage set. (316) The long, zigzag ramp at the UNESCO in Paris from the lower garden to the upper level. The sense of choreography is very strong and the masonry walls are immediate and tactile as you walk by them.

The most pleasant ramp is on a slope of 5 per cent, which is to say, 1 foot rise for every 20 feet in length. However, a rise of 1 foot in 10 is readily negotiable and more frequently used. On short quick ramps, a rise of one in seven is permissible though tiring, and should usually be guarded by a railing along the path.

(317) A ramp both for vehicles and pedestrians looping around the back of the Paris opera house. (318) Assisi, an Italian hill town distinguished by its infallible use of levels as the very essence of its civic design.

317

318

319

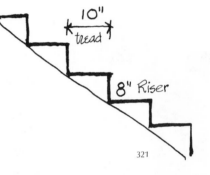

320

321

(319-321) The relationship of step risers to treads is vital to the ease and comfort of negotiating the flight. If the proportions are poor, the kinesthetic experience can be unpleasant, even, at times, dangerous. The point to remember is that outdoor steps require a different proportion than those indoors, largely because the scale of striding and walking is different. The usual indoor rule of thumb is that twice the riser plus the tread should equal 25". Outdoors, the resultant must be 26 for the most common steps, but this increases to 28" for broader flights; a 5" riser, for example, often used in broad, slight shifts in elevation, will require an 18" tread. (See 305.)

BOLLARDS

322

323

Small scaled sculptures called bollasters or, more commonly, bollards are used to channel movement on ramps and streets and to exclude wheeled vehicles in a polite way. They do not say "Stay out," they say, "Come in on your feet." (322) Italy. (323) Spain.

324

325

326

327

328

329

(324) Pisa. (325) Rome. (326) England. (327-329) United States.

FENCES

Three examples of extreme politeness in civic design. The transparent fences allow the passerby to look through and enjoy the view without permitting intrusion. (330) Spain. (331) San Francisco. (332) A glimpse into the sculpture court at the Museum of Modern Art in New York City.

331

332

WALLS

(333, 334) Barriers must sometimes be more solid. The screening wall between the main plaza of Capital Towers, a residential development in Sacramento, open to the public and heavily trafficked by pedestrians, screens off a recreation area from noise and view. It has been treated as a great frieze, cast in concrete by the sculptor Jacques Overhoff and tilted into place.

333

334

335

The vertical surfaces of buildings and freestanding walls can bring architecture into intimate contact with its users. By modulating the surface, using it as a canvas for works of art, or modeling it as sculpture, the wall gains another dimension and achieves a sense of scale, texture and shadow pattern which makes it interesting for the passerby. (335) Concrete cast in styrofoam molds by Overhoff. (336) Sandcasting by Virginia Davidson.

336

337

(337) Hebrew University entrance, Israel, by Danziger. (338) Tile walls at UNESCO by Joan Miro. (339) Brick wall by Henry Moore in Rotterdam. (340) Artist unknown.

340

338

339

341

WATER IN

There is a quality about water which calls to the most deep rooted and atavistic part of our nature. In the deep canyons of our cities, water, along with fire, trees, and the almost hidden sky above, are the elements which can still tie us to our primitive past. Of all these, water and fire evoke the most direct responses. Fire in the city is dangerous, negative and evil; while water is positive and life-giving—the element from which we all have come. The wildness and exuberance of water stirs us with its qualities of nonconformity and vigor. Even in the captive, contained, and confined pools of our urban waterways, water affects us in the same way as does a wild animal in a zoo, pacing back and forth in his cage, beautiful and quietly desperate, controlled but with implications of wild danger. Water reminds us of high mountains and streams, of deep chasms and gurgling brooks and the quiet sounds of the wilderness. Even in a city, the sound and sight of water stirs the most elemental and basic roots of our human natures.

For centuries, men have brought water into their cities for aesthetic displays as well as for drinking and bathing. The earliest water courses in the cities of the East were channels for irrigation, running down from the mountains along the curb lines of the streets into cool, green, gardens enclosed by walls. On their way, they watered the palms and citrus groves, and cooled the air by their sound as much as their evaporative sprays.

Each culture since then has had a strongly expressed attitude about water and the way it has been used; in each period the greatest inventiveness and highest talents have been lavished on the intricate and exciting use of water. In Persia and the Middle East, water was treated in flat pools, brimming full and almost running over like wine in a goblet. The edges of these pools have always been carefully

THE SQUARE

sculpted and controlled, so that the container was architectonic and carried the major design impact. The water was used for its reflective qualities and its cool implications. Even the jets here (and later in the Spanish gardens derived from these) were only thin tinkling streams.

The water gardens of Italy were more exuberant and active. Starting high in mountain streams, the water was brought in across country in flumes, running hard and swift into the upper courses of the terraced slopes, and then these pressures were channeled into hundreds of different effects—waterfalls, great jets, cascades, sprays from walls, even surprise fountains which wet unsuspecting guests at parties. The Italian civic fountain appeared in every square and every piazza, usually combined with sculpture, in a never-ending, fascinating interplay of marble and water, so often so baroquely intertwined as to make it difficult to discover which was more active, the figures or the water.

The waters of France were quieter sheets—great, reflective, symmetrically organized and curbed basins; their control—like the control of their trees and ground planes—expressed the French attitude about nature. To be beautiful, natural elements had to be controlled. The Japanese attitude was diametrically opposed to this. Each pool was a miniature of nature; each stream concealed its source; each lake was surrounded by hills and rocks as an expression of the essence of wildness—the ineffable quality of man's relation to wilderness in capsule.

In our own time, the advances of modern technology have opened great new possibilities for the use of exciting water effects in our cities. One of the most difficult and trying considerations, that of bringing in adequate water supplies, has been overcome by the new pumping systems. Louis the Fourteenth assigned three thousand Swiss mercenaries to dig canals to bring water for the fountains of Versailles. They worked for two years, half of them died from malaria, and the fountains could still only be turned on for special occasions. Our new recirculating pumps have overcome all these difficulties and have made it possible to re-use the original supply of water without any loss or refilling, and in any amounts desired. In addition, control valves and jet sizes, orifices, and shapes now can be fabricated in an innumerable variety of types and sizes designed to produce any desired hydraulic effect.

The most recent advance of all is in the programming of changing water effects. By the use of the new time-clocks, tape devices, electronic controls, and computers, the most elaborate and complex mobility and change in water effects can be carefully programmed and controlled. These water effects can be interwoven with sound and lighting into a new and multidimensioned series of fascinating relationships, which can be involved or simple, and which consist no longer of water alone, but of a vast kaleidoscope of diverse elements. There is real danger, however, of losing sight of the inherent quality of water in these exuberant amusements—of that very quality of chance which water brings to us. When we control too much, we have lost the great virtues of unpredictability and have made instead a static form out of a wild and mobile element.

(341) At the Villa d'Este near Rome. (342) One of Bernini's twin bowls at St. Peter's, Rome.

342

QUIET WATERS

Quiet, still waters mirror the city for us so that we see both the actuality and its image.
(343) The Kampen, Holland, with its beautiful 18th century houses along the tree-lined canal. (344) A long reflecting pool in an office courtyard, Hayward, California. The surrounding buildings are mirrored in its quiet surface.

344

345

GUSHING WATERS

346

The turbulent, gushing quality of water develops both a sense of visual turmoil and a roar of sound.
(345) At the Villa d'Este outside Rome—a landscape created with water. (346) The fountain of Gefion and her oxen in Copenhagen—an ancient myth expressed in bronze and gushing water.

(347) Khaju bridge and dam at Isfahan, Iran. This great civic monument takes a functional necessity and lifts it into the realm of high art. The steps below the bridge echo in their form the waves of the river which they channel. Julian Huxley gives the legendary history of the bridge in *From an Antique Land:* "Shah Abbas told his architect that the bridge must fulfil many functions beyond that of carrying traffic. It was to provide repose: so in each pier there had to be a stair leading down to a restroom with couches. There was to be a space for wedding parties (the bridge is still used for such festive celebrations); and a retreat for a holy man; and rooms where singers and dancers and jugglers could entertain travellers. Furthermore, the Shah insisted that even in summer, men's ears should be charmed by the sound of running water; so the architect made a special channel to collect every trickle of dry-season water into a sufficient stream. And when the bridge was finished the Shah visited it disguised in every capacity to satisfy himself that his instructions had been carried out. Only then was the architect paid." (From an article by Elizabeth B. Kassler in *Architectural Record*, June 1959).

347

348

349

Water has great recreational uses as well as visual ones, even in the city. (348) A swimming pool used primarily by young people. The floor of the pool has been inlaid with glass mosaic. (349) Along the Seine. Right in the heart of the city relaxation is possible, and a whole day can be spent along the river. In addition, there are walks, fishing, paintings to make and picnics to enjoy.

(350) A modern version of the old swimming hole in a neighborhood park, Spokane, Washington. (351) Water has endless fascination for children.

351

350

352

353

354

The visual qualities of water depend largely on its activation and the way it reflects light. (352) It has luminosity and brilliance, and when caught in droplets, it sparkles like gems. (354) As it falls, it moves the flat surfaces into ripples and corrugations, and these reflect the light with pinpoints of brilliance. (353) Depending on the light which strikes the surface, it can be dull and leaden.

QUALITIES OF WATER

356

357

355

Water has sounds as well. It gurgles, it splashes. (355) It goes plop, plop, plop. (356) And fshzzzsh. (357) And spaatzzz! (358) The quality of water cooleth on a hot summer day.

358

RUNNING WATER

From the earliest times, irrigation ditches in ancient lands carried the water along the sides of the streets. (359) Avenue in a developing section of Teheran.

(360) A channel at the Villa Lante, Bagnaia, Italy, carrying the water from upper levels to lower ones in gradual leaps. The form of the walls of the channel echoes the movement of the water and squeezes it at nodes where it then leaps into small waterfalls. (361) In a water garden in Hillsborough, California, the surface of the water is broken up and aerated by the small square inserts which break the water surface as it passes.

362

363

When water falls, its surface is broken and aerated and it becomes luminous and alive.
(362) The waterfall at the Villa d'Este. (363) A small fall between two channels. The design of the lip of the container serrates the water into a series of five threads.

364

(364) Sheet flow over a steel edge. (365) A water stair in a garden. The sound of the water is as important as its visual qualities, for at each step there is a gurgle which creates a Doppler-like effect.

366

The edges over which water flows control the effect. (366)
Prismatic surfaces break up the water and aerate it. (367)
Serration channels the water into droplets.

367

EDGES

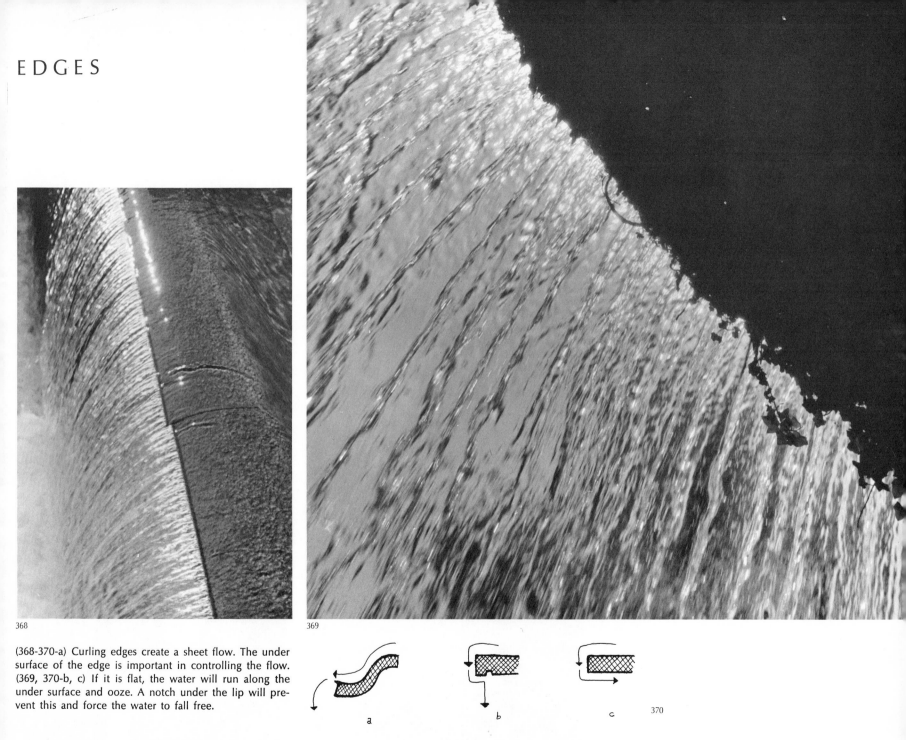

368

369

(368-370-a) Curling edges create a sheet flow. The under surface of the edge is important in controlling the flow. (369, 370-b, c) If it is flat, the water will run along the under surface and ooze. A notch under the lip will prevent this and force the water to fall free.

a   b   c   370

371

The great excitement of jets is that they defy gravity and explode into the air. This is the most unnatural of all the uses of water, and one of the most dramatic. (371) A series of small jets forming a curtain of water. (372) Jets used instead of plant forms contrast with the hard surfaces of concrete walls.

372

150 WATER IN THE SQUARE

JETS

(373) The great 300' high Jet d'eau in Lake Geneva. (374) A 150' high jet of water with a ring of satellites. The orifice is 3" across; the pump is delivering 2,000 gallons per minute with 155 horsepower. Mount Rainier is in the distance.

373

374

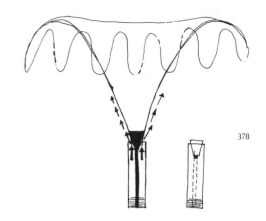

378

375

377

379

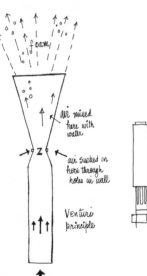

376

The form of the jet, the shape of the orifice, and the pressure with which the water is squeezed through the jet all control the final effect. (375, 376) Aerated jets. Air is mixed with the incoming water so as to create a foaming effect. (377, 378) Mushroom jets. The position of the plunger controls the height and extent of the mushroom. (379) Bubble fountain, Tivoli Gardens in Copenhagen. The aerating effect is reversed in these jets; the water is contained within the glass columns and air bubbles are moved through the water.

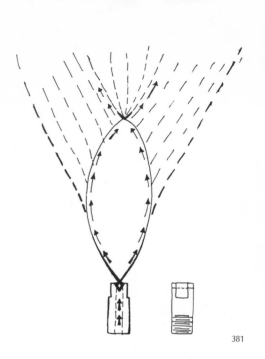

(380, 381) A peacock tail—achieved through the use of an industrial sprinkler normally used in cooling towers.

382

BOWLS

The bowl is the simplest form of sculpture with water. It can lift water up high in a square without resource to great pressures; it can increase the feeling of water without the need for large volumes; it can serve as a source for a waterfall or stand in a plaza as a piece of sculpture. (382) In front of the Società di Navigazione in Genoa. (383) In the courtyard of the Sevilla Cathedral. (384) Graceful bowl in a Granada courtyard.

383

384

386

387

385

388

389

390

(385) Some specially spun copper bowls in a small pool. (386) Library courtyard at the Hebrew University in Jerusalem—a concrete casting related to the sun shade capping the building. (387) Bowl, Berkeley, California. (388) The John Hancock roof deck fountain, a single 12-foot square of black granite. (389) A flower form made of three identical precast sections, Oakland, California. (390) In the courtyard of the U.S. Science Pavilion, Seattle World's Fair.

391

If a pool has great depth, it reflects the color of the sky and the water appears blue; but if the pool is shallow, as in most decorative fountains, then the water is colorless and the bottom surface is seen and becomes important. (391) In the bottom of a long runnel, inserts of varicolored river washed stones set a pattern which echoes the movement of the water. (392) A swimming pool enlivened by a colorful glass mosaic by Ray Rice.

392

393

(393) The terrace paving of native pink limestone has
been carried from the terrace down the steps and into the
bottom of this pool, Hadassah-Hebrew University Medical
Center, Jerusalem.

SCULPTURE WITH WATER

(394) A brilliant bronze sculpture by James Fitzgerald at the Fine Arts courtyard at the Seattle World's Fair. The abstract qualities of the sculpture and the movement of the water are interlaced into a complex composition of water and metal.

The baroque way with water was to add water to sculpture, so as to endow the marble with great qualities of movement. (395) A latter-day baroque fountain by Carl Milles in St. Louis. (396) Villa d'Este. (397) The great Trevi Fountain, Rome, which creates in its small square a whole complex world peopled by gods and waterfalls. (398) The organic approach to water.

395

396

397

398

PROGRAMMING

(399) Score for fountain, Seminary South Shopping Center, Fort Worth. A visual method for programming water effects is necessary when designing a complex series of events. The system here illustrated was developed by the author to make this possible. Each group of jets is drawn as a graph separately, and the height is plotted against time. Under each are the secondary effects notated with specially designed symbols which indicate sound, surface characteristics, shape of droplets, etc. Finally, the various jet groupings are combined together in the top graph as a means of relating them all together in an orchestral effect.

399

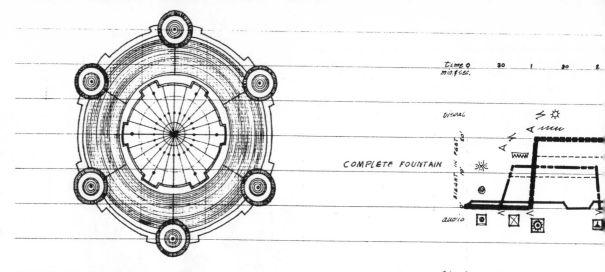

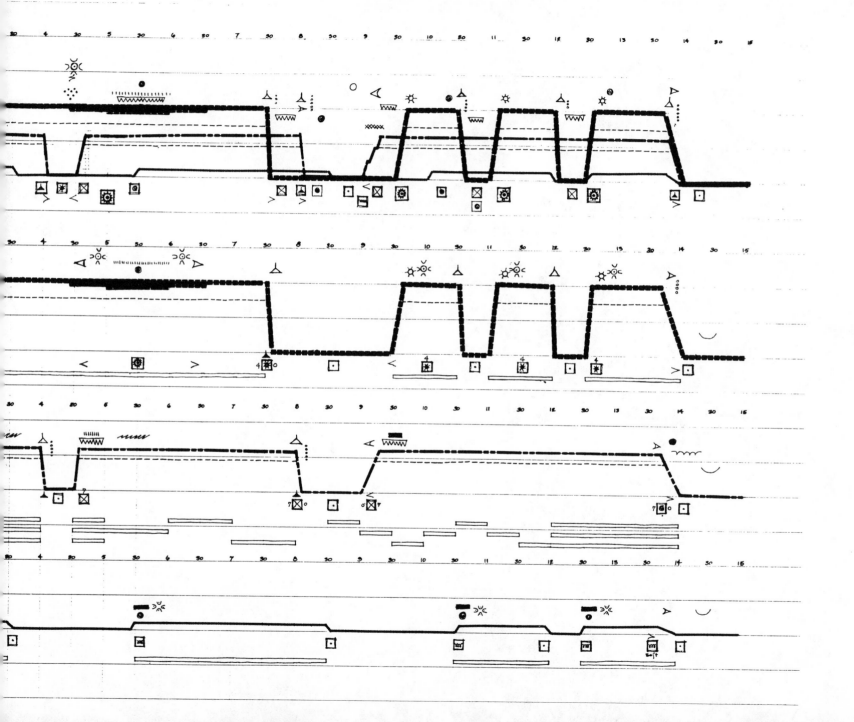

TREES FOR ALL SEASONS

There is an old Chinese proverb which says: "No shade tree? Blame not the sun but yourself."

Trees are a vital part of a city. They give people a contact with nature, establish a relationship with primitive needs and soften the hard, unyielding surfaces of urban construction with the green of leaves, texture, and shadow. In addition, they perform a real physiological function in removing carbon dioxide from the air and replacing it with needed oxygen.

Throughout history, designers have had two differing attitudes toward the planting of trees. Long before Le Notre made his beautiful gardens in France, trees were planted architectonically. In Persia, in ancient Egypt, and in India, trees were grouped formally in precise rows, which derived from the linear qualities of irrigation systems. French gardens were equally orderly, but for different reasons. Theirs was a play of spaces which *used* trees: trees pleached as high hedges or pollarded for continuous canopies; orange trees in huge pots; *parterres de broderies* carpeting the grounds (401). To these designers, plants were materials which they employed in the careful delineation of spaces, not because they loved or even respected nature, but because they enjoyed domination over her.

The other landscape attitude in history has been romantic, soft, naturalistic—trees used as organic forms, untrimmed, unpruned, left to grow naturally in clumps or groupings, simulating as much as possible the grouping of trees in natural woodlands. In this tradition are Chinese and Japanese gardens (402), the romantic effusions of the English landscape, Capability Brown's eighteenth-century clumps of trees in the English countryside. Our large parks in this country owe their designs mostly to this romantic attitude, but our plazas and street trees hark back to the planting of Versailles and Egypt.

401

402

DESIGN

Whichever groupings seem appropriate, there are several basic physical demands which become clear in inserting trees in the cityscape. Street trees are normally planted 25 to 40 feet apart, but this often has to be varied a great deal to conform to buried utility lines, driveways, light standards, building entrances. Sometimes trees can be planted much closer together, especially if they are kept fed and trimmed. Plantings in rows 10 feet apart, or in bosques, create a handsome canopy, strongly massed and most effective in establishing a street facade of trees. Trees in plazas and small parks have much more flexibility in their placement. Groupings in bosques, either pollarded or pleached, can define a space far more successfully than the linear quality of trees in rows. Treated as high hedges, they enclose spaces as walls of green; grouped, they can be organized carefully into symmetrical architectonic masses or placed loosely in a green square.

(403) Aix en Provence, Cours Mirabeau—a double row of elms planted 20 feet on center. (404) The same street at eye level. In the distance is a fountain.

405

406

407

(405) Versailles, one of the cross axes. (406) Champs de Mars, Paris, in summer. (407) Champs de Mars, winter aspect, showing light pollarding of trees.

408

409

(408) Grosse Promenade, Mainz. The high hedges are horn-beams. (409) Tuileries, Paris. The pleached hornbeams echo the facade of the buildings.

166   TREES FOR ALL SEASONS

410

411

(410) Ailanthus in a small square off the Grand Canal in Venice. In the distance, a charming kiosk. (411) A square in Giron, Colombia. One tree makes the square.

412

(412) Tivoli Gardens in the heart of Copenhagen. A fine grouping of natural plant forms. Willow and maple are the dominant trees. (413) Roehampton, London. A housing development built in an old estate. The trees have been carefully preserved and maintain a park-like atmosphere for the inhabitants. (414) This Berlin street is called "The Birdsong." A unique example of tree planting using only one type of tree—European White Birch—which has established a strong and poetic quality.

(415) The planting of sycamores in front of the U. S. Science Pavilion, Seattle World's Fair, is in the same character as the Gothic tracery of the man-made arches by Minoru Yamasaki.

413

414

415 —

PRUNING

416

(416) Heavily pollarded trees in a completely paved space at Berkeley, California. (417 a, b) Technique of pruning. (418 a, b, c) Physiology of tree; watering and fertilizing.

There are, however, specific and difficult conditions the tree in the city faces which are directly opposite to its natural environment.

In the deep woods, trees lead a tranquil life. Leaves fall and mulch the ground, protecting the roots. Aging wood also falls and decays, increasing the organic content of the soil. Because of high transpiration (emission of water vapor from the leaves), a relatively high humidity is built up. The air is pure and clear, and the transpiration through leaf pores is constant and unimpeded. There is group protection from winds in the forest to prevent excessive drying. The natural filtered shade is advantageous for the growth of seedlings, keeping them from being baked by the hot, dry sun. Animals deposit fertilizers, the ground is spongy and absorbent, and rains are easily retained so that the moisture necessary for the intake of foods is stored. Birds and air currents disseminate the tree seeds and help establish a plant community whose ecology is quite perfectly balanced.

The tree in the city, however, has an almost wholly hostile environment. The roots are completely covered by pavement; no water or air can reach them, and plant foods are inaccessible. Through venturi action on city streets, they are often subjected to cold, drying winds and drafts. Planted singly, they cannot protect each other.

City air is poisoned by gas fumes, smoke, heavy deposits of soot, smog, coal dust, which coat the leaves, preventing transpiration and the absorption of carbon dioxide from which the leaves manufacture food through photosynthesis. Residues from these deleterious chemicals concentrate on the leaves and in the soil, creating destructive effects. This is harmful, not only to trees, but to humans as well. But the trees cannot escape to the country on weekends, nor can they retreat into a controlled air-conditioned environment of their own choosing.

In spite of these difficulties, trees *can* be successfully planted in urban conditions. With proper care and understanding of their needs, we can make successful urban green belts, streets lined with trees, parkways, and small urban parks to help soften the overwhelming scale of hard, unyielding materials in our cities. The urban tree, however, has to be carefully chosen for hardness, recuperative powers, and all-around toughness. In addition, careful attention to the physiology and technical requirements of city trees—care in planting, maintenance, and feeding—is essential in the inevitable battle to keep the toughest trees alive and thriving (418 a, b, c).

City trees demand pruning, the selective removal of wood. At the outset, when transplanting, it is wise to remove about one-third to one-quarter of the tree's wood to reduce water loss through the leaves, since the roots are unable to offset this loss. This is major: one oak tree gives off 120 tons of water through its leaves per year. Pruning can also achieve architectonic qualities and keep trees within limited city sizes.

Even after a good strong start, city trees can triumph only if they get tender loving care consistently. Trees need to be watered, sprayed, and extravagantly admired.

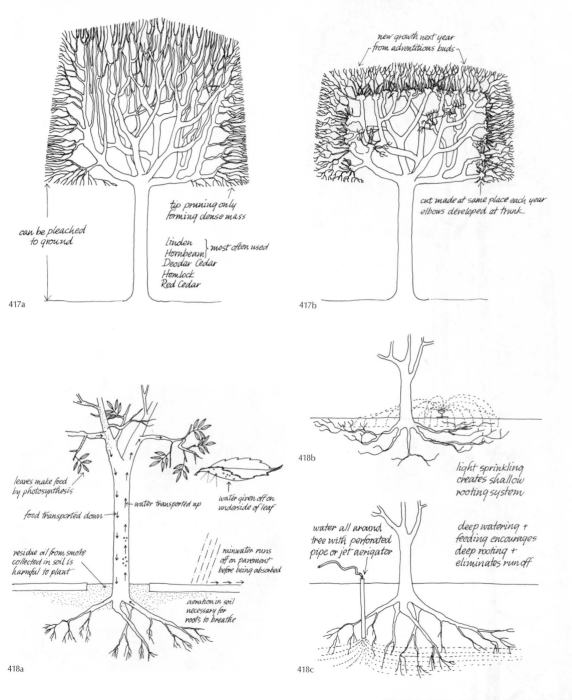

417a

can be pleached to ground

tip pruning only forming dense mass

Linden
Hornbeam } most often used
Deodar Cedar
Hemlock
Red Cedar

417b

new growth next year from adventitious buds

cut made at same place each year elbows developed at trunk

418a

leaves make food by photosynthesis

food transported down

water transported up

water given off on underside of leaf

residue oil from smoke collected in soil is harmful to plant

rainwater runs off on pavement before being absorbed

aeration in soil necessary for roots to breathe

418b

light sprinkling creates shallow rooting system

418c

water all around tree with perforated pipe or jet aerigator

deep watering + feeding encourages deep rooting + eliminates run off

PLANTING

(419) In transplanting trees, points to be considered are as follows: First, measure and specify sizes correctly. Size of a tree is indicated by caliper, height, and ball size, i.e., 6 inch caliper, 24 feet high, 6 foot ball. Normally the ball size in feet equals the caliper of the trunk in inches. Second, compute the weight of the ball to anticipate handling problems. (420) To do this, square the diameter of the ball (in inches); multiply by the depth of ball (again in inches); subtract one third from the total; multiply the total by .075. For example, a 3-foot ball, 30 inches deep, will weigh 1944 pounds.

$$36^2 \times 30 = 38880$$

$$38880 - \frac{38880}{3} = 25920 \qquad 25920 \times .075 = 1944$$

The best size for normal planting is 2- to 3-inch caliper and 10- to 12-feet high. These trees are large enough to be seen, but do not suffer great shock in moving. However, where special immediate effects are desired full sized trees can be planted if given careful handling. For these large trees (6 to 10-inch caliper, 30 to 35 feet high) the ball size should be 6 to 10 feet in diameter.

420

419

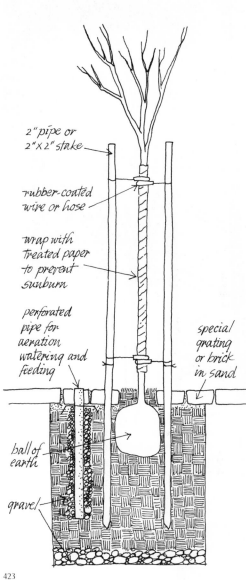

2" pipe or
2" x 2" stake

rubber-coated
wire or hose

wrap with
treated paper
to prevent
sunburn

perforated
pipe for
aeration
watering and
feeding

special
grating
or brick
in sand

ball of
earth

gravel

421

422

423

After transplanting trees, they should be wrapped to prevent sunscald, and following this, they should be guarded with tree guards to prevent vandalism. (421, 422) Both examples are in Paris. (423) Proper procedures for planting and maintaining young trees in the city.

424

425

426

427

Trees on city streets or in plazas require devices for aerating the roots and allowing water to seep into the surrounding soil. These devices become an important element in the floorscape and can be highly decorative as well as purposeful.

(424) Granite blocks in the main shopping area at Stevenage New Town at the base of some existing trees. (425) Precast concrete sections surrounding the base of a newly planted tree in a pedestrian mall, Berkeley. (426) Precast concrete in a plaza of exposed aggregate concrete, Palo Alto. (427) Granite setts surround an iron grating, Washington, D. C. (428) The famous Parisian cast iron grating.

428 →

a. Acer platanoides — Norway Maple. A wide round-headed, densely foliaged tree. Leaves are five-lobed, quite large, and deep green, turning a golden yellow in the fall. A fine tree for a symmetrical, clean, impenetrable look. Height 40 feet, spread 35 feet.

429a

b. Aesculus hippocastanum — Horse Chestnut. The famous tree which grows on the Champs Elysees. The flowers bloom like white candles in May, coming out with the lovers. A wonderful tree with a handsome, five-fingered leaf, it grows up to 50 feet high with a 30-foot spread.

429b

429c

c. Ailanthus altissima—Chinese Tree of Heaven. The tree that grows in Brooklyn will grow anywhere. It has a fine tropical quality and handsome fruits which hang in clusters. Thin, very often multistemmed, finely divided leaves. Height 40 feet, spread 35 feet.

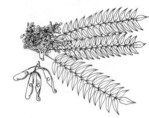

d. Carpinus betulus—European Hornbeam. A fine tree for shearing and pleaching. This was the tree used mostly in Versailles for the high hedges pleached down the allees. A small, elegant leaf and a clean, upright, black-barked trunk. Height 35 feet, spread 25 feet.

429d

429e

e. Fraxinus pennsylvanica lanceolata — Green Ash. A good, all-around, tough, vigorous tree. The bark is most interesting: marked diagonally, and quite black in color. Height 35 feet, spread 30 feet.

429f

f. Ginkgo biloba—Maidenhair Tree. A living fossil which owes its life to the fact that it has been planted for centuries in the temple gardens of China. The females of this species produce evil-smelling fruits, so use only the male. Height 60 feet, spread 35 feet.

TREES FOR USE IN THE CITY

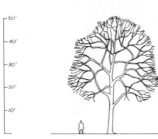

429g

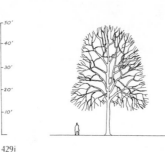

429h

429i

g. Gleditsia triacanthos – Honey Locust. Very high-headed, spreading, umbrella-shaped tree with a beautiful silhouette, deep black bark, and fine textured leaves. Tough and handsome. Height 50 feet, spread 40 feet.

h. Platanus acerifolia–London Plane Tree, Sycamore. The most planted street tree in North America. It can be sheared, pleached, or pollarded with excellent effects, withstands winds and soot admirably. Other excellent sycamores: Platanus orientalis–the Oriental Plane Tree, Platanus racemosa–the California Plane Tree. Height 50 feet, spread 40 feet.

i. Quercus borealis–Red Oak. The best of the oaks for city conditions, clean, handsome, upright, and all-American. A deeply serrated leaf which turns a brilliant red in the fall. Height 50 feet, spread 40 feet.

j. Salix babylonica–Weeping Willow. Actually a native of China, this willow is not good for a street tree but is wonderful for small parks, playgrounds, backyard gardens. Its long, yellow, whiplike twigs have a fine color when the leaves have fallen. Height 30 feet, spread 30 feet.

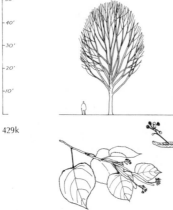

429j

429k

429l

k. Tilia cordata–Linden Basswood. The famous "Unter den Linden" tree, an extremely popular street tree in Europe. A beautiful round shape, handsome heart-shaped leaves, and delightful small flowers. The American species, Tilia americana (called basswood), makes some of the tastiest honey in the world. Height 50 feet, spread 30 feet.

l. Zelkova serrata – Japanese Zelkova. Very much like the American elm in its shape and leaf, though smaller, and can be used in its place since it is not susceptible to the Dutch elm disease. Height 45 feet, spread 50 feet.

THE VIEW FROM THE ROOF

Without his garden on the roof, David would never have found Bathsheba. And ever since, the view from the roof has been important to the city dweller. The hanging gardens of Babylon (431), the promenade along the city wall in the moonlight, the rooftop gardens of India and Persia and the middle East have been among the greatest amenities possible in cities from earliest times.

Rooftop gardens give a dimension to modern city living which is impossible on the ground. Up high on the roof there are views over other buildings, sunsets to see, a relaxing freedom from cars and other traffic, a privacy and intimacy which no other city facility can bring and all of which are difficult to achieve at street level. As our modern cities build higher, and as open spaces become more difficult to acquire, the use of the open space on the roof—which normally is wasteland—becomes more imperative (430). The simplest roof garden is a small balcony where a person can step outside into the open air and stretch, and grow the potted geranium which keeps him aware of growing things; it can do much to ameliorate the claustrophobia which city living imposes.

But the true roof garden can go much further than this. If it is properly designed it can provide all the elements of a ground level garden: it can catch the warmth of the sun, protect people from winds, point toward distant views, and give a very special flavor to outdoor living. And if it is designed initially as part of the structural system of the building, there are few limits to the plants, trees, and even fountains which can be placed on it. There is, of course, a certain limit to the depth of soil one can pile on a roof because of weight factors. Since wet soil must be computed at 110 pounds per cubic foot, this does pose special problems in roof gardening. These are mostly connected with inadequate depths of soil for

431

430

the growth of large trees and also the rapid evaporation of water from the soil, since no great capillary action can bring deep waters up from below. However, other than the careful selection of types of trees and shrubs from those able to survive in shallow soil and a careful maintenance program of watering, spraying and fertilizing, gardening on roofs has few special requirements or limitations. Almost any beautiful garden can be enjoyed on a roof.

433

LIVING ROOM

434

(432-436) A roof deck garden on Telegraph Hill in San Francisco overlooking the bay. The size is 32 by 44 feet. The usual gravel on tar roof was enriched by a careful selection of handsome beach stones to maintain the vernacular but add interest. Where outdoor walking, sitting, and entertaining occurs, wood duck boards set on sleepers serve as a smooth and lightweight surface. Because of the wood frame construction and earthquake problems, depths and weights of planting beds were kept to a minimum, and shallow boxes with drought-resistant plants were used.

435

436

437

(437-441) An old warehouse in San Francisco has been converted into a workshop for the author's design group. Windows and doors were punched through the concrete walls, disclosing magnificent views of the city, and a simple wood deck built on the existing roof has added an enormous dimension of use and enjoyment. The warehouse quality has been kept through the use of old electric cable spools and timbers, and this former waste land has become an important extension of the indoor space.

438

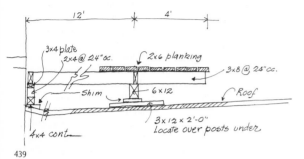

439

440

441

(442-446) In the very heart of San Francisco, the 14-story tower of the John Hancock Building by Skidmore, Owings & Merrill, was set back from the side property lines to preserve light and air. Because of the setback a roof deck became possible, to which all executive offices open. The roof deck is overlooked by all the upper story offices. Since this is a new concrete structure, it was possible to use far greater loads than either of the roof gardens on the previous four pages. A green rug of lawn was sown on 12" of lightweight soil; trees and hedges in mounds and raised boxes add a dimensional quality to the flat surfaces. The fountain is a single 12' square slab of black granite from the quarries of Minnesota, and the paving stones are travertine. Views of the buildings across the street were carefully preserved so as to maintain an urbane and enclosed quality to the space and provide a contrast in architectural time with the elegance of this modern building.

442

443

444

446 →

PUBLIC

(447, 448) A roof garden on a new garage at the pre-earthquake Fairmont Hotel in San Francisco. A place for fountains, dancing, and views across the city. The palm trees which recall the Victorian era when the hotel was built, are planted in great sunken pits especially designed and suspended between the beams of the underground garage. The Victorian love of carpet bedding—the combination of low-growing flowers, leafy plants, and colored gravels arranged in complex patterns—has been carried into a modern design.

448

(449-451) Santa Monica Redevelopment Project, a new community, designed specifically for the automobile. An underground, multi-storied garage steps upward in the form of a ziggurat, forming a series of terraces upon which the houses and outdoor gardens have been placed. This is a modern hanging garden related to the early ones in Babylon in its form and search for amenity. All the houses have direct access by staircases and bridges to the hidden automobiles at their own level (designed by Demars and Reay, Architects).

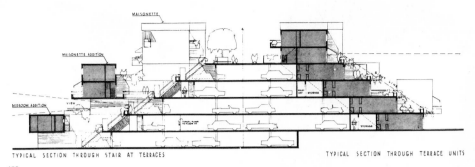

TYPICAL SECTION THROUGH STAIR AT TERRACES   TYPICAL SECTION THROUGH TERRACE UNITS

450

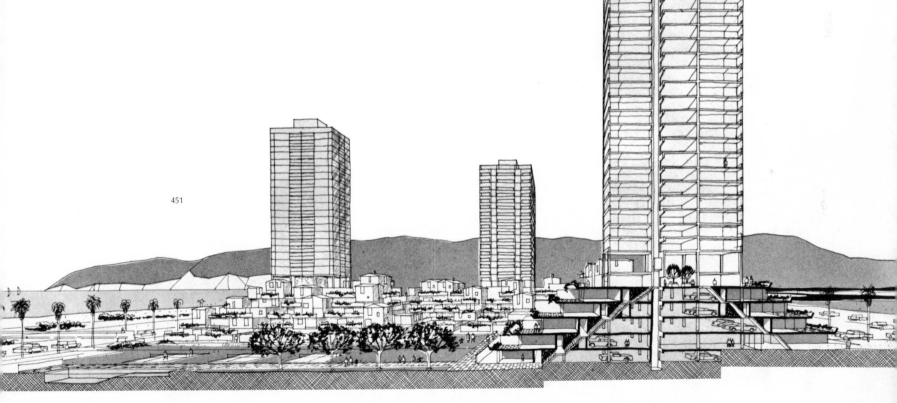

451

← 449

452

190 THE VIEW FROM THE ROOF

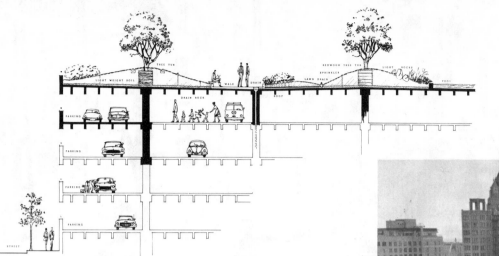

453

GARAGE TOPS

(452) This appalling picture of the center of an American city illustrates in capsule the urban design dilemma of our times. At least half of this valuable area is devoted to streets and parking lots which intrude like cavities in the fabric of the city. (453, 454) The one encouraging note is the garage for the Kaiser Building, whose roof deck, designed by Osmundson & Staley, has brought a delightful green space into this wasteland.

454

CHOREOGRAPHY

Participation and activity are essential factors in a city. One can be a passive spectator in the enjoyment of other arts, but the essential characteristic of the city as an art form is that it demands participation; it requires movement through its spaces. A city is a complex, many-dimensioned elaboration of structures and spaces organized into rhythmical juxtapositions where events happen. And a city must be experienced through movement to come alive in its most unique sense.

As an environment for choreography, many dimensions must be considered in the city. First is the dimension of speed. The quality of a city sensed by moving about at the speed of a pedestrian—a maximum of four miles per hour—is vastly different from that at faster speeds. At pedestrian speed, all the elements and details which we have described come into sharp focus. Floor, ramps, steps and other minor shifts in elevation exert a physical impact, and the furniture in the street is directly at hand and personally experienced. The process of sitting in a sidewalk cafe, the spatial qualities of great squares, the shopping street as a heavily crisscrossed area—all are experienced by the pedestrian who moves about the city at a pace of his own choosing.

While walking in the city down a quiet street, the surroundings are comparatively static. Buildings and objects move past at a slow speed and the effect is relatively quiet and unhurried. Objects are seen in the same position long enough so that their relationship is clearly established and perceptible. The cross movements and staccato qualities arise only from other pedestrians who establish movement patterns of their own. The crisscross sense of overlappings comes mainly from these opposings and crossings, and they create eddies of motion, like water currents in a river.

At certain times, pedestrian movements become vastly more active. They vary greatly with the time of day and the intensity of activity. Shopping areas or meeting places are usually full of the most vibrant movement, and the streets can become so full of activity that a pedestrian must adopt a defensive attitude of watchful walking, so as not to bump into others or be himself knocked off his feet.

People have different rhythms of moving while walking, and the sense of their own gestures is varied and noticeably different. The variations are individual, it is true. Each person moves differently and has his own particular signature in his movement. But rhythmic movement also varies with cultural backgrounds and patterns, and the movement of national groups in a city vary considerably one from the other. This is most noticeable as one moves from one neighborhood to another in a city, particularly when national groups have maintained their own identities. It is particularly noticeable when people are traveling away from home; an American in Paris is more distinctive by his method of walking than by any other characteristic. The places for pedestrians to move around in should be designed both for their activities and their kinesthetic characteristics.

The type and design of space has a vital influence on choreography. Long linear vistas, overly great spaces, undifferentiated and uninterrupted streets, lack of color are dull and uninteresting, not so much because of their static visual qualities but because they are uninviting to move through at pedestrian speeds. If they become too uniformly dull, they achieve a nightmarish quality of personal disassociation; they are impossible for a person to relate to. If he finds no fixed intervals, or changes, or points of interest, he will even choose *not* to walk through these amorphous kinds of spaces.

456

455

457

PEDESTRIANS

On the other hand, an active environment with many closely placed, small-scaled objects of great interest can become frenetic even at slow speeds, because the person on foot finds them visually too complex and exciting. They can force the pedestrian to slow his speed by their very complexity. Active and interesting shop windows are a good example of this phenomenon; their detail and pull can be designed so as to practically force pedestrians to stop and look and "window shop."

The design of urban spaces for pedestrians should be thought of in terms of the person in motion, and the environment through which he passes should be designed to fulfill specific functions. This is a fact well known to merchants and store designers, whose careful evaluation of pedestrian movement geared to salesmanship could well be studied by urban designers. Shopping center developers, for example, have made careful studies of pedestrian tendencies, and among other things, have established width criteria for streets based on impulse shopping habits. In addition, they know the typical pedestrian pattern of right-hand movement down a street, and its relation to the positioning of store fronts and entrances. In contrast to this was the static, axially-oriented point of view popular in Renaissance and Beaux Arts planning (457). Their spaces were all laid out as if viewed in perspective from a fixed point. Cities, as well as paintings, were designed to be seen from one place in a one point perspective, as if movement did not exist. But this is giving way in our time to the understanding of the changing point of view, the mobile, non-fixed ever-shifting viewpoint (459). Even when designing for pedestrians who move at comparatively slow speeds, the environment relates to the person constantly in motion with a varied viewpoint and a constantly changing position.

(458 a, b) The shopping street as evaluated by a shopping center developer. The offsets provide excellent merchandising frontage as long as they are in the view of normal pedestrian movement. If they occur counter to the movement, they generate dead space, which is difficult to rent because visually inaccessible. The 40 foot width is optimum for impulse buying because it generates cross street movement unless the street is much wider and other features occupy the center.

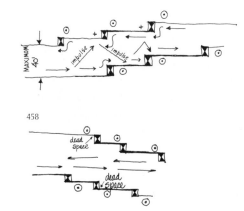

458

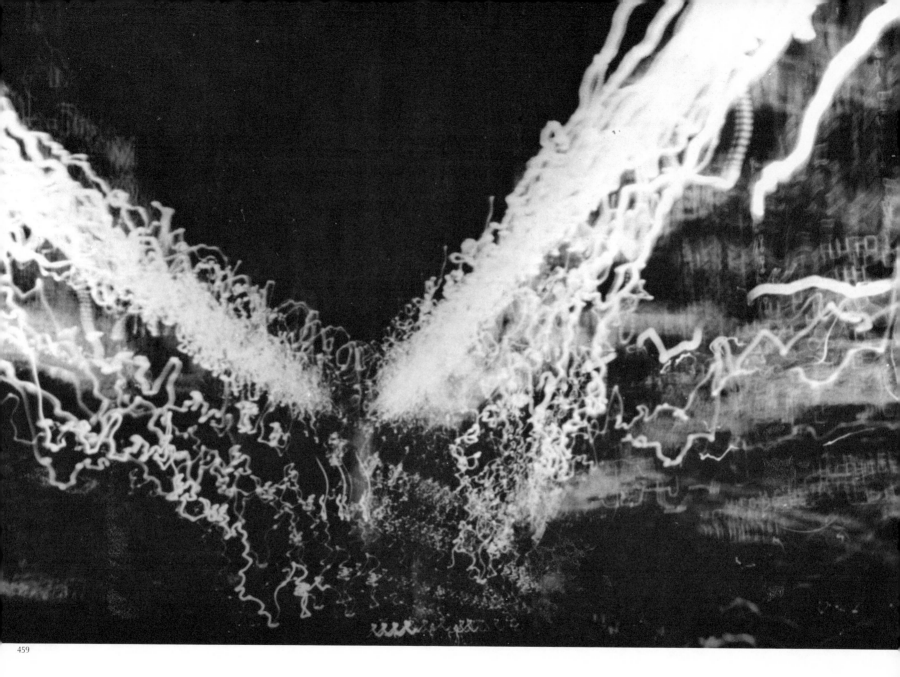

459

460

461

The essence of our urban experiences is the process of movement through a sequential and variegated series of spaces.

Thus, the beautiful street is beautiful—not only because of the fixed objects which line it—but also because of the meaningful relationships it generates for the person-in-motion. His movement is the purpose for the space, and it should function to activate his kinesthetic experience in a series of interesting rhythms and variations in speed and force. The qualities of moving up and down on ramps and steps, of passing under arches and through buildings, of narrowing and widening of spaces, of long and closed views, of stopping and starting are qualities which make a vital urban experience for the walker and his mobile point of view.

Painters have been working for some time with this shift in attitude toward a mobile, rather than fixed, viewpoint. Picasso's paintings of multifaceted faces, showing various aspects of a person at the same time, were an early attempt to convert this simultaneity into a fixed moment frozen in time (460). And the futurists based their experiments on the notion of movement. More important to this approach, perhaps, are the spidery paintings and drawings of the action painters, whose intricate spatterings and elaborate overlappings of web-like lines convey to the observer a sensation of moving points traveling rapidly through spaces of vast depths and complexity (461). The sense of speed can here be grasped as an endless track through the painted surface, the lines as a tracery of motion. Photographs of people or objects in motion disclose the same characteristics as these paintings (462, 463).

462

463

AUTOMOBILES & FREEWAYS

The automobile has introduced another, more compulsive dimension of speed into the city than the pedestrian, and mobility is even more with us. The visual experience of viewing a city skyline from platforms strung high over the streets, at the speed of 65 miles an hour, adds a whole new quality of experience in viewing the city, and opens up a whole new series of relationships for the city dweller. The skyline becomes more important to the motorist than for the pedestrian, not as a static image, but as a mobile, ever-changing series of overlapping images, superimposed one next to another, almost like a moving picture. Close-in detail gives way to large-scale impressions, telescoped in time and space, and different in impact. The great scale of the city as a gigantic functioning organism becomes more apparent; detail is lost and the strength of large scale landmarks and geographic forms becomes significant.

While driving a car, the mobile viewpoint actually becomes physically essential (464, 465). Here, the ever-shifting relationship to surroundings is more frenetic; adjustment to shifts in speed and position in relation to other moving objects is more demanding and more dangerous. As a result, design for movement becomes a function of safety, and not only a matter of aesthetics. In high speed freeway design, motion is the most compelling requirement, and engineers have learned well the close relation between alignments, curve radii and transitions, and the impact they have on safe design speeds. Our engineering standards on roads are excellent. What highway designers have yet to take adequately into consideration is the relation of road design to the environment, the visual images seen and felt beyond the road, the road's impact on the surroundings through which it moves.

465

← 464

The problem in handsome freeway design has been thought to be primarily one of the design of structures, but this has been overemphasized. Most freeways, no matter how beautifully structured, cannot overcome the enormous damage and destruction which these vast and complex arteries cause in the heart of a city by their very presence and, more importantly, by the fact of their dumping cars into the downtown core. The real problem is how to integrate freeways into the fabric of the city without destroying important civic values. It is the fragmentation of outlook, and inadequate attention to integrated overall environmental planning, rather than the architectural design of the structures, that has resulted in serious errors. It is impossible to think that the sole concern of freeways is to bring automobiles quickly into cities with no concern for aesthetics, environmental impact or scale. In the process of a singleminded approach to mobility, every other aspect of environmental design has been sacrificed, as though speed and mobility were the only and ultimate justification, with an overriding virtue of their own. As a result, freeways have cut great swaths through urban communities, whole neighborhoods have been sliced in half, parks have been segmented, waterfronts have been cut off from the body of the city, and the intricate, closely woven texture of the city's tapestry has been demolished (466). The visual impact of the concrete ribbons, often beautiful and well designed in themselves, has been responsible, over and over again, for the destruction of every other urban value except speed. It is a sacrifice hardly worth the cost.

The complexity of integrating freeway design and other modes of travel into the whole urban environment must take many different solutions (467). The most obvious and hopeful is to completely bar the automobile from the city core. Ultimately, I believe, we will have to come to grips with the notion that cars cannot come into the city, or by sheer numbers

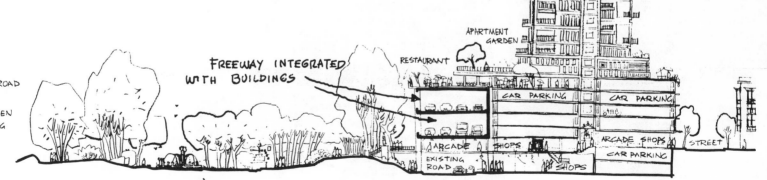

FREEWAY INTEGRATED WITH BUILDINGS

APARTMENT GARDEN

RESTAURANT

CAR PARKING   CAR PARKING

ARCADE   SHOPS   ARCADE SHOPS   STREET

EXISTING ROAD   CAR PARKING

SHOPS

STRIP PARK

1 BLOCK

FREEWAY OVER EXISTING ROAD
DEVELOP BLOCK
APARTMENTS, ROOF GARDEN
RESTAURANT, CAR PARKING
SHOPS & ARCADES

467

468

they will destroy the very essence of downtown.

We could, I am sure, apply by analogy the Malthusian theory of overpopulation to the automobile (468, 469). Instead, we will have to develop comfortable, high-speed rapid transit systems, which move more people more quickly in and about the city and cause less destruction to its fabric, as has been begun in Sweden at Vallingby. But this does not answer all needs nor provide all choices. Some freeways will be necessary, but they need not necessarily be destructive if they are meshed into the fabric of cities in sensitive ways, with an understanding that other values must have priority.

The design of urban freeways on the whole, must follow a design approach which is diametrically opposite to rules laid down for scenic highways out in the country. The scenic highway should be gently winding. It should follow the contours in a continuously unfolding sinuous series of interwoven horizontal curves, and constantly rise and fall with the natural configurations of the countryside. Normally, to be aesthetically pleasing, a very wide right-of-way is desirable out in the country, with wide median strips, gently rounded slopes on embankments and easy transitions on the verges. If these criteria are applied in the heart of cities, they result in havoc. The long, sinuous curve destroys innumerable houses, the wide right-of-way creates barriers of incredible width between neighborhoods, and the continuous curves are completely unsympathetic and visually destructive to the predominant linear qualities of the city. The scenic highway in the city is anti-urban and destructive of urban values. Urban freeways must be designed as part of the urban environment, with narrower rights of way, linear qualities, and multiple levels; they must employ structural and urban qualities, not rural or romantic ones.

470

471

(470) The monorail installed for the Seattle World's Fair. It is rapid and quiet, and the light rails do not darken the street. (471) As a permanent installation, the station could be in a building and need not overshadow a pedestrian square. The main point, however, is that it is fun to ride on, and therefore was extremely successful financially during the Fair. The mass transit systems of the future must make the experience of riding an enjoyable adventure (as do the cable cars in San Francisco); otherwise they can not compete with the automobile and will not be used.

Freeways can, in places, become part of the structural systems of cities by making them an integral part of buildings, or by actually building structures over them. They can run under and over parks, even at great heights, in the same way that bridges leap across rivers, high enough so that the blight implicit in their shadows is removed. Ultimately, too, they can, in cities at all events, be designed for slower speed standards, so that the long, sweeping curve, which takes up great spaces, can give way to the sharper curve, which forces slower speeds easier to integrate into civic design. If freeways are elevated, what happens underneath them becomes paramount. Instead of the present offal of parking lots and corporation yards, bus depots and cyclone fences (472), the ground underneath should be devoted to parks, greenways, and pedestrian open spaces, so that the freeway becomes a generator of amenity, rather than a blight (473). Parking can be done in special structures designed for this purpose, in designated locations on the fringes of the core, so that automobiles do not penetrate into the heart of the city. The essential point is that amenities in a city *must* have priority over the automobile at whatever the cost to mobility.

It is important to make a difference between qualities of speed of movement through space. Our problems in cities begin when streets for pedestrians and those designed for automobiles—the one designed for small-scale, very detailed and close-in and leisurely experiences, and the other for high speed transit—interfere with each other and are used at cross purposes. The square and plaza where leisurely activities occur—sidewalk cafes, theatrical and musical events, sculpture exhibits and meetings—is no place for high speed throughways bearing automobiles. One needs to differentiate in cities, just as in private living quarters, between functions and speeds and their hierarchy of importance.

473

(474) An early proposal for the separation of pedestrians and wheeled vehicles in New York. The drawing from *L'Illustration*, 1874, shows the system, a short portion of which was built. The raised platform is a moving sidewalk designed to carry people and small drawing rooms around the city at a speed of 15 miles per hour. The smaller cabs on the side tracks, by slowing down, would enable passengers to leave the moving walk safely.

The simplest differentiation in speed can occur through differences in level, and the most obvious device to separate pedestrians and automobiles is to put them at different heights in a city. The new local street, choreographically designed, will be multileveled—the machines at ground level, rapid transit at a still lower level, and pedestrians raised above both, on upper decks and bridges closer to the sky and free from the dangers and impediments of high speed vehicles.

475

(475) Early pedestrian bridge, Savannah, Georgia.

476

(476) The Golden Gateway Development in San Francisco now under construction. The different types of mobility are well expressed and envelop the area. In the distance is the freeway, and the off ramps dive into underground garages. The dwelling units are all built up on the roofs of two-story parking structures, and pedestrian bridges connect this pedestrian level across the city streets. An excellent example of an automobile-oriented urban development.

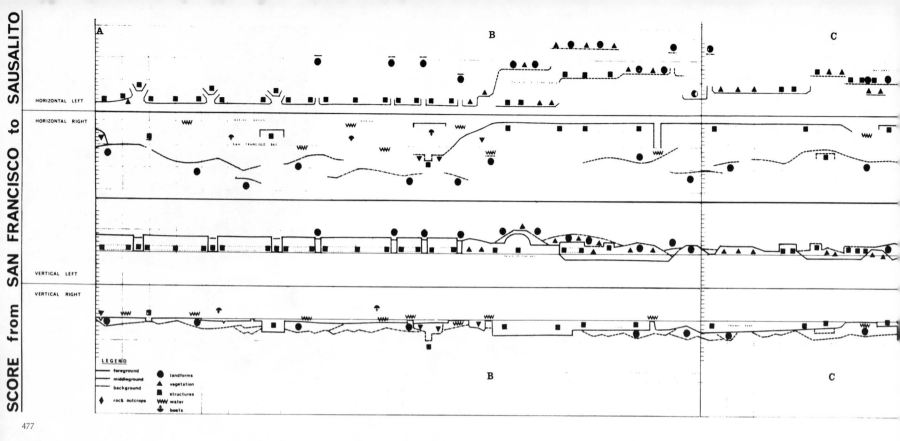

HORIZONTAL LEFT

HORIZONTAL RIGHT

VERTICAL LEFT

VERTICAL RIGHT

LEGEND
foreground
middleground
background
rock outcrops

● landforms
▲ vegetation
■ structures
〜 water
⚓ boats

477

MOVEMENT NOTATION

In order to design for movement, a whole new system of conceptualizing must be undertaken. Our present systems of design and planning are inevitably limited by our techniques of conceptualizing and our methods of symbolizing ideas. We know only how to delineate static objects, and so that is all we do. Since we have developed techniques for showing buildings and objects, and outlining the spaces which they confine, we plan by architectural symbols, projected in conventional methods, on paper. We use the plan and the elevation, the isometric projection, and sometimes a model. But all these accepted systems of architectural language describe only the fixed surroundings, the structures and the spaces which they enclose. Landscape plans, which tend to be less rigid and exacting, are still limited to a description of plants as static phenomena, or of the hard masonry structures in the environment. This limitation of symbols affects our results. Since we have no technique for describing the activity that occurs within spaces or within buildings, we cannot adequately plan for it, and the activity comes, in a sense, as a by-product after the fact. It is true that any good designer or planner will *think*, while he is designing, of the activity that eventually will occur within his spaces. But he cannot design the movement, for he has no tools to do so. Even highway engineers who deal with movement have no method of describing it.

A new system should be able to focus primarily on movement, and only secondarily on the environment. This would have use as a technique for designers working kinesthetically. Though many painters have painted action, they, naturally, have always been completely qualitative and subjective and have not

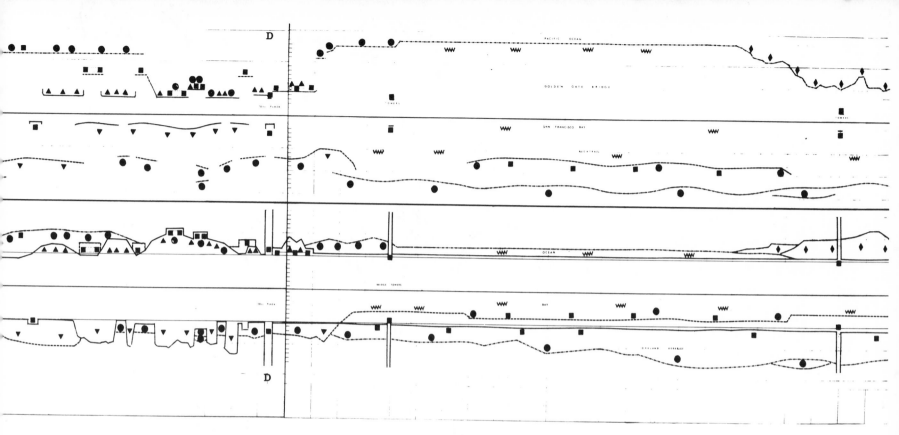

intended to codify a transmittable or universally understandable system. We need a system to program movement carefully and analyze it, a system which will allow us to schedule it on a quantitative as well as qualitative basis. Since movement and the complex interrelations which it generates are an essential part of the life of a city, urban design should have the choice of starting from movement as the core—the essential element of the plan. Only after programming the movement and graphically expressing it, should the environment—an envelope within which movement takes place—be designed. The environment exists for the purpose of movement.

In an attempt to describe motion through space I have developed a simple system which has been a useful tool for this purpose.

In the drawing above (477) and on pages 212, 213

the focus is on the action as a moving line, the environment is described secondarily and the technical device is a simple one. It resembles, basically, the fixed position of a ship delineated on a radar scope, with other objects always plotted relatively to the ship as the center. But in this case, the center is drawn as a moving horizontal line and the projected environment is plotted at right angles to right and left. The drawing uses conventional scales and time intervals and, once studies are completed, may be ultimately converted into architectural plans and elevations or engineering layouts. It can be used to program designs and to decide, by plotting a sequence of motions, the elements of interaction in the environment. It has use as a tool for visualization, a method in one's mind's eye, of walking, running or driving at a certain speed through an environment of

The lights hanging from the center of the arches on the outside are apparently an
afterthought -- they are crackled like Sam Hurst suggested for College of the desert &
have a hole in the middle -- they look extremely well! the lights down the center
do not give enuf' light. The sense of movement in the square is enormous & exciting !!

Piazza San Marco - Venezia
Friday July 14

478

one's own selection. It can be used to conceive of events taking place in space during a period of time, to notate happenings, and to extend our ability to evolve an environment of new dimensions—of interactions and interrelations. It is a new tool for choreographing in the city.

The elements of mobility in a city, however, go far beyond the man-oriented ones and we should be aware of them and plan for them. Even in a city, animals have a life full of motion; birds are even more mobile than we are. The Piazza San Marco in Venice has become a stage set for its pigeons (478), which crisscross the sky in a series of incredibly involved choreographic patterns. And the greatest delight for visitors is to stand in the square, hands outstretched, and coax the birds to flutter closer and closer 'til they land on their hands to feed amidst a beating of wings. Cities are full of dogs who are out in the street and in the plazas scurrying about (479), and the parks are full of squirrels and chipmunks, darting here and there.

The sense of water in the city and our great empathy with it is in no small measure related to the qualities of motion, both visual and audible. Fountains are exciting to us because they move and gyrate; cascades fall and the spray of droplets, caught like streaks of light in the sun, are the very essence of motion traced through their trajectory. The motion of fountains and the qualities of water effects can be programmed by an extension of the system I have described for motion in space (pages 160, 161). Here, however, the sense of sound and the qualities which water generates, as it spills over ledges or activates still surfaces are important and require their own emphasis in the notation system.

479

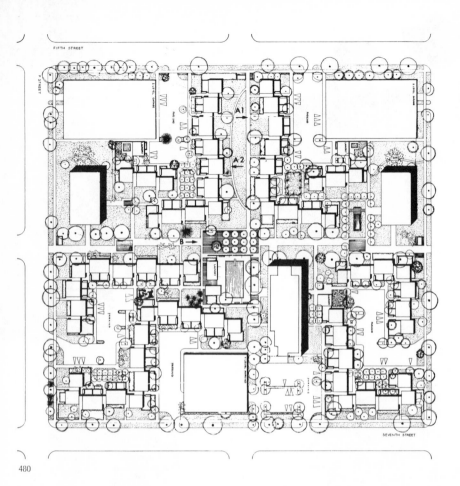

480

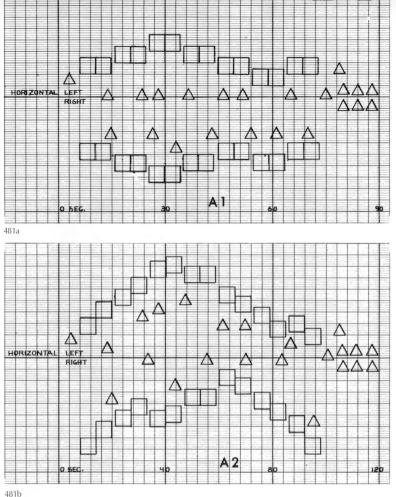

481a

481b

(480, 481a, b, c) The plan is of a four-square block area in Sacramento recently rebuilt as the first living space to follow the redevelopment process. The automobile is confined to peripheral areas; the center provides for pedestrian walks, gardens, recreation area, and a plaza at the core. The notation system here is used to evaluate the walking experience in two areas. The "main track" plots the planimetric path of the moving person and relates him to the fixed objects in the space. The sequence is then recorded on horizontal and vertical tracks which mark these relationships, plotting time and distance. On the horizontal track, objects to the right are in front of the path and those to the left are behind. In reading the tracks, bear in mind

that the basis of the system is that the environment is moving and the person is fixed. The area marked A, a space between two groups of houses, can be traversed on either the straight path A1, or the curved path A2. The plaza area is designated B. The notation B1 indicates the experience of walking directly through the plaza; B2 indicates a more leisurely experience—walking around the plaza to the sculptured fountain, sitting on a bench, and then on. In both cases, the variegated experience encountered in the nonlinear patterns A2 and B2 are readily observable through the notation system. This is an example of an evaluation of a given design. But the system also functions conversely to develop designs for kinesthetic experience.

○ FOUNTAIN

△ TREE

▭ BENCH

▬ WALL

▭▭ BUILDING

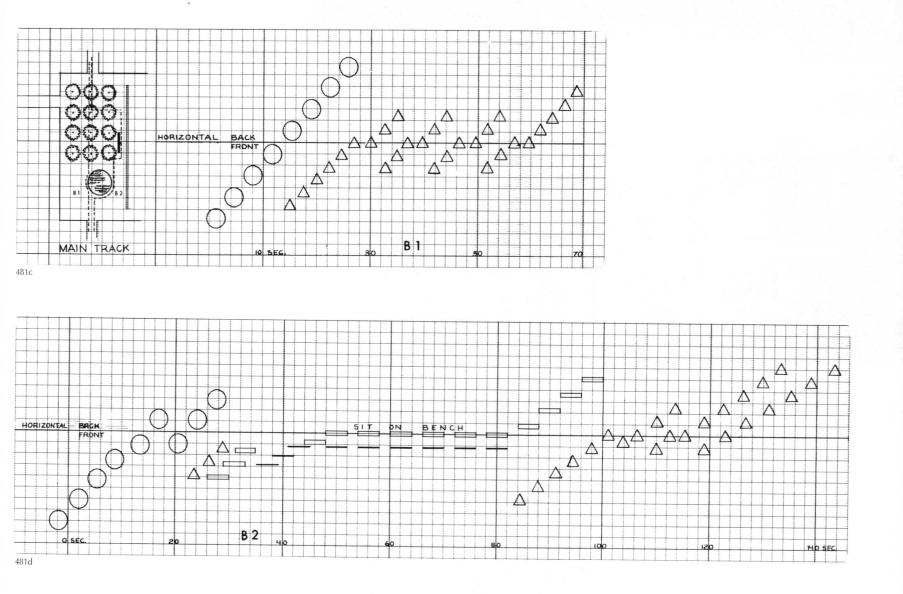

481c

HORIZONTAL BACK
FRONT

MAIN TRACK

B 1

10 SEC.   30   50   70

481d

HORIZONTAL BACK
FRONT

SIT ON BENCH

B 2

0 SEC.   20   40   60   80   100   120   140 SEC.

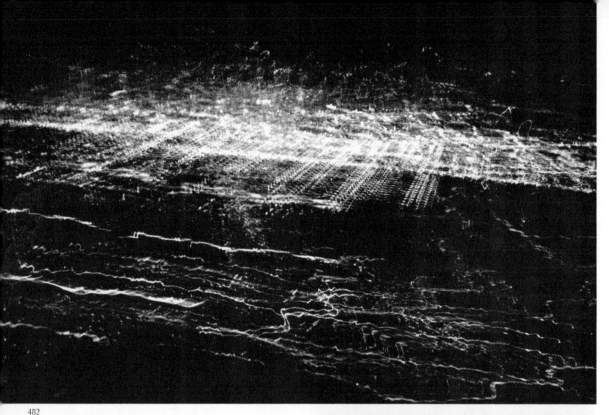

482

483

The mobility extends up to the sky, which, even in a city, has qualities of constant movement. Clouds incessantly cross our vision, moving with the wind and intersecting one another in a variety of patterns, both in form and color. The greatest kaleidoscopic display, of course, occurs at sunrise and sunset when the colors pulsate and change in an almost liquid interchange of dazzling displays. And one of the great joys of living or working up high is the great views of the ever changing qualities of the clouds.

Other movements occur in time rather than space, and these are the processes of change. The most constant of these are the changes of seasons—those great cyclical events which occur year after year and have such profound effects on all aspects of existence. The fact is, of course, that this is caused by movement—the great revolution of the earth around the sun in its yearly orbit. A city looks and feels different during the different seasons. In winter under now, it may be sparse, pure, and quiet; much of the dirt and grime is covered over. To be in Paris in the spring is one of the greatest human experiences in the world; when the white blooms on the great horse chestnuts light up like candelabras and the lovers are intertwined in the Bois de Boulogne. Summer in a city can be hot, muggy, and uncomfortable, and most people want to get out of cities during these months. The change and pulsating rhythmic variation in seasons imposes a cyclical quality to life in the city, equally as strong as in the country. One of the clearest functions of trees and planting in the city is the quality of seasonal change to which they bring biological emphasis. In most cities, the trees are deciduous, and the seasonal emphasis is strengthened by their changes. Early spring brings the swelling of buds, then flowers, and the clean fresh green of the new leaves. Finally, in northern climates, the brilliant reds and yellows of autumn color give way to the bare, black branches and twigs silhouetted against winter skies.

The diurnal movement is more startling in its quality of change, but because it occurs daily it seems less obvious. From sunlight to darkness is a change as dramatic as one can conceive, and the whole aspect of a city and a city's life shifts from one part of the day to another. The face of life changes, the kinds of activities change, and, of course, the whole visual qualities of a city's physiognomy shift from day to night. The most exciting views of cities are at night. From heights of 30,000 feet they are seen as a blaze of multicolored, flickering lights (482), and the earth becomes a rhythmic interplay between great patches of dark, unseen farmlands and uninhabited areas, punctuated at intervals by the warm glow of city lights coming up sparkling in the dark voids. City patterns are clearest at night; outlying residential areas are faintly lit and the incandescent lights are dim and widely spaced, glowing warmly in the grids of the street. The shopping streets blaze out

stronger; they are bright and multicolored; the neon glow seen from great heights sends long brilliantly-colored linear gashes through the body of the city, intersecting at the crossings and the important centers into great colorful explosions like the pinwheels of fireworks.

Down in the streets, at pedestrian level, the city at night comes alive with moving lights and a whole kaleidoscope of events begins. The lights move and gyrate. The tall buildings at dusk begin to pulsate with lights whose pattern is never fixed but randomly activated (depending on the number of occupants who happen to be there), causing a chance turning on of lights in a non-synchronized pattern (483). The most fascinating rhythms can be seen by watching groups of skyscrapers at dusk, as the intermittent sequence of lights comes on in a series of chance designs. These rhythmic relations seem to affect the

people in the street. More activity starts. In the heart of the city, at the centers of amusement and night entertainment, whole streets are lit into a blaze of light. One experiences this as if in the center of a light mobile (484), whose pulsating movements surround the viewer in an environment of neon, a collage of activity and excitement. As a result, pedestrian movements seem to become faster and more intense, and the whole structure of the rhythms of a city increases in its tempo and syncopation.

Sunday morning is quiet. Down the long, quiet, canyons the tall buildings stand empty and resting. The pace of motion has stopped and the noise in the street is still. One can hear the echo of footsteps on the paving, where normally the street is so full of sound that a shout cannot be heard. The tempo of events has stopped and the city is calm and still. There is little, if any, movement.

484

CHANGE

Change, over long periods of time, affects the structural makeup of the city. Its configuration changes, like a forest where trees age and fall to the ground, to be replaced by younger, more active, saplings. As in a forest, too, fire can rage through a city; earthquakes or other natural phenomena can affect its structural form. A city, like a forest, is a delicately balanced ecosystem, always in transition. The city's structures, of course, are buildings rather than trees, its plazas are like clearings in the woods. But age affects buildings, too. They become ancient because they become outmoded for their functions, rather than aged in the biologic sense. And when they no longer perform their functions, they are felled like great trees and newer, brasher ones take their place.

But some buildings and places need to be preserved in a city for reasons beyond the purely functional. We need, in cities, buildings of different ages, reflecting the taste and culture of different periods, reminding us of our past as well as our future. Some buildings are beautiful or striking enough to have their useful periods artificially extended by preservation—almost like seed trees in a forest—so that succeeding generations can enjoy them, and through them maintain a sense of continuity with the past. Old buildings and old sections of cities establish a character, a flavor of their own, which often becomes the most interesting and provocative part of a city. Part of this is due to scale, since each age develops its own sense of scale and relationship of

(485) The history of Grand Central at a glance. This great monument to civic design, which took the enormously complex problem of bringing large numbers of trains into the very heart of New York City and solved it by skillful manipulation of levels and underground concourses, also presented a magnificent terminus to Park Avenue.

485

486 487

parts. In addition, technologies change, and even within the span of a generation buildings become aged in their style and design attitudes, affecting strongly the qualities of a neighborhood. One of the most difficult and sensitive architectural design problems is to improve an older building so as to continue its usefulness while maintaining its initial character and flavor. Unfortunately, our main streets in America are full of hideous examples of handsome old buildings which have been desecrated under the name of modernization (488).

More important, however, than the character and flavor old buildings lend to a city is our very human need for old buildings whose rents are low and spaces are large. Unfortunately, we don't seem to be able to build the kind of large disheveled space with good light so necessary for the artist and the sculptor. Or, indeed, for that matter, for the old pensioner with four dogs who can pay only a modest rent. The old building or warehouse can give us that higgledy-piggledy space which lends itself to remodeling and to the off-beat demands of some of our most important citizens. A sculptor friend has said to me that a remodeled slum is the perfect place to work; for it is inexpensive, has great character, and with its exterior wash lines it is a great inspiration to artistry. The billowing shapes of colorful laundry between buildings are, he says, halfway between flags of protest and flags of victory.

488

(486, 487) show this great landmark overwhelmed and demeaned by the immensity of the new Pan Am building, which in addition to dwarfing this significant building, adds a permanent population of 17,000 workers and 250,-000 daily users to an already overcrowded area.

489

SKYLINE

The impact of change, when it comes, is felt most on the skyline. In older times the rate of change in a city was slower and more leisurely, and the skyline grew carefully. There were also accepted patterns of architectural importance which found their outward signs in the heights of buildings. Churches were most important and their silhouettes dominated the skyline. The "duomo" in the Italian city rose like a symbol above everything else. By convention, if not by law, the Italian city was dominated by the physical presence of the church (489). All other buildings were subservient to this; everywhere you walked in the city, the church rose as a central dominating element, giving a sense of place and centrality to the composition. And from afar, the white dome always rose over the countryside. Next in the hierarchy of importance and, therefore, heights, were the civic buildings, the town hall, the burgher's offices and finally the towers of the richer citizens. It was a carefully organized and stable hierarchy, whose outward forms echoed its inner workings; as a result, the silhouette of the city remained stable for centuries.

Now our skylines change overnight. Great skeletons rear up on the hills overnight, topping one another in height and mass, each new one dwarfing the scale of the next and cutting the views of its neighbors. In our times the hierarchy has been reversed and the office block dominates (490), followed by the high-rise apartments, and finally the civic buildings and the churches. In our times the gem-like public buildings are the small ones, whose importance is almost indicated by their tiny size in comparison to their immense neighbors.

But our real problem lies in the rate of change and the accelerating pace of new constructions which constantly shifts the character and outline of the city's silhouette. We have few valid mechanisms for controlling this change and little to guide us in ways to shape this important image of the city. What we do know is that change has become the essential element of our time. The static conception of society and its image in the city has given way to a conception of fluidity, of constant change. Our great mission is, I believe, to deal with change, to recognize it as an essential element in our time and accept its implications. Since our ideal form for the city is uncertain, what we need to strive for is an environment designed for the process of creative living. In the search for this environment, the acceptance of the process of change as the essential basis for civic design will signify our understanding of the problems and uncertainties of our technological future. There is no way to plan creatively for a static society or a static environment, neither of which any longer exists. Every attempt to do so implies a rigidity of control and a narrowness of aim. These will result in visual sterility, or politically in an imposed and overly-controlled society whose citizens become insect-like and dehumanized. There is no rule book for guiding change except to recognize its importance and welcome it as a challenge.

490 →

A city is a natural phenomenon as well as a work of art in the environment. Form in nature is not a result of preconceived order. It evolves as it grows or happens, as mountains develop by upthrusting, boulders by glacial dropping. An art form to me is a result of the inherent nature of materials and the process of putting them together. The art of urban design, as other branches of modern art, follows a naturalistic process. The designer does not give form to a preconceived idea, he takes the elements and allows them to come together. In the process of their coming together, he finds new relationships between things, and only then does he exercise control by making selections. The form evolves as the total process is in progress. The search for form is a search for valid processes.

EPILOGUE

Some ten years ago the first edition of this book was written. It has gone through a series of reprints but now for the first time is being produced as a new edition. I am delighted that this newer edition is being published by the M.I.T. Press in paperback because that will result in a lower cost, thus making the book available to a wider group of people and particularly to students who have for some time used the book as a reference text.

This new edition makes it possible to add to the original version sixteen pages of recent work, thus bringing it up to date so to speak and, more importantly, showing actual completed examples of many of the theories and ideas originally expressed but not completely tested at that time.

The examples I have chosen for illustration here are in San Francisco, Portland, and Minneapolis, and each emphasizes one or another major point about urban design. Ghirardelli Square emphasizes the importance of preserving old and valuable landmarks in cities and converting them to new uses—architectural rejuvenation. It also demonstrates how older, run-down, and previously under-used sections of cities can be revitalized and in the process spark a whole new surge of activity. That was achieved by converting an old chocolate factory into a new area of shops, restaurants, theaters, and a multiplicity of other uses without demolishing an entire neighborhood and building anew. Old and new are meshed together to the mutual advantage of each.

Nicollet Avenue in Minneapolis shows how the decaying main street of a major city can become an urbane, enjoyable, and economically viable boulevard within a very short time. Once Nicollet was rebuilt, almost overnight the entire downtown became rejuvenated, and major constructions on both sides of the avenue have begun all along its length. In this example both public and private initiative joined hands in the rebuilding of the street—the city and downtown merchants jointly sparked the effort that has revitalized downtown Minneapolis. One of the major factors in this revitalization has been the removal of private automobiles from the street and its conversion to a bus-oriented transit way.

The removal of the automobile from large enough sections of cities seems to be a major first step in bringing life back into downtown. Once that is done, as in Nicollet Avenue, a whole series of opportunities becomes available. Then the pedestrian is freed from the tyranny of noise and fumes and the physically overwhelming presence of cars and traffic. In this sense the Embarcadero Plaza in San Francisco became possible only when this terminus of Market Street was closed from traffic and the area converted to a four-acre park and plaza. Until then this major focus of the city served only as a convergence of streets, and automobiles occupied the entire space. Once it was converted to a pedestrian zone, an entire new life-style could be developed: a major plaza surrounded by hotels came into being—shops, a vast new building complex, a great environmental water event, grass, trees, outdoor eating areas and cafes for thousands to enjoy daily.

The Portland fountains have made a major impact on their city for several reasons. They initiated the idea of environmental sculpture—in motion as something you use and become involved with. This overcame the standard idea of civic art as appealing only to the visual senses and the notion of monumentality as being inhuman in scale and function. Here function and symbolic image were linked, and citizens were literally invited to use their civic art; thus it becomes part of them and they a part of it in an act of *collective fantasy*. Perhaps even more important, however, is the pedestrian-oriented open-space network lacing the city, of which these water plazas form one part. The whole network (not yet entirely completed) extends for many blocks. These plazas and green parks are connected by pedestrian walkways to which shops and restaurants are linked. Along the malls, private gardens, office courtyards, shopping areas, the civic auditorium, hotels and apartment buildings, and townhouses are all joined together in an intricate and varied series of multiple-use open spaces.

These examples demonstrate a cardinal fact about our existing cities: they *are* retrievable and *can* be made enjoyable and exciting to be in and participate in, in addition to being economically viable. They also show that all aspects of urban design are significant and that we need not destroy a city to have it rise like a phoenix from the ashes. We can insert beauty wherever and whenever it is feasible—from the lowliest catch basin to the grandest water plaza or street. The art of Cities is an art of creative assemblage and change requiring the constant and energetic input of all its citizens. It is, in the grandest sense, a participatory environmental art without boundaries.

——Lawrence Halprin, March 1972

GHIRARDELLI SQUARE

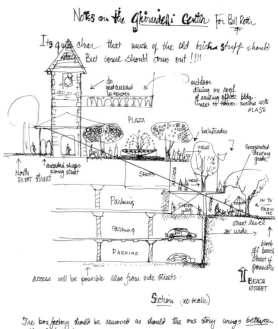

Notes on the *Ghirardelli Center* For Bill Roth

It is quite clear that much of the old brick stuff should. But some should come out !!!!

Section (no scale)

The box factory should be removed as should the one story wings between the old factories.

A great plaza at the upper level should be developed — around it a "BEEHIVE OF EXCITEMENT" with several

493

In their original form, Ghirardelli's brick buildings housed a famous old Italian family's chocolate factory (494). The tower brought images from the old country to the New World. Ghirardelli today, converted to new uses, preserves the traditional landmark tower and puts the old buildings to new uses.

The drawing above describes the first conception (493) as proposed by the author to William Roth, the enlightened developer who conceived Ghirardelli Square. Parking is dug out underground, and a series of rising levels of terraces and open spaces cascades down the "hill." There is a cacophony of uses—many restaurants, innumerable shops, theaters, galleries, movie houses, and displays (492). The sensitive architectural remodeling is by Wurster, Bernardi & Emmons.

494

495

496

497

498

499

(494–499) In addition to its multiplicity of uses, Ghirardelli Square was designed to be fun to be in. One of the great achievements is "people watching," and young and old come here to sit in the sun, eat in the different restaurants, listen to music, and watch each other. The many levels are connected by steps and ramps and balconies and are filled with places to sit, plantings, fountains, and sculpture. In the distance are views of the bay, and cars are excluded.

NICOLLET AVENUE

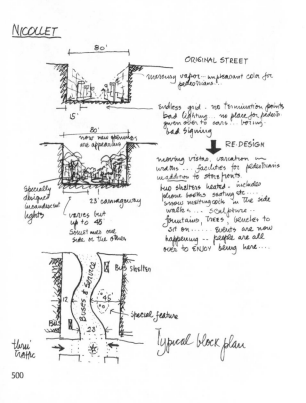

NICOLLET

ORIGINAL STREET

mercury vapor... unpleasant color for pedestrians...

endless grid - no termination points
bad lighting... no place for pedests.
given over to cars... boring.
bad signing

⬇ RE-DESIGN

moving vistas, variation in
widths... facilities for pedestrians
in addition to store fronts.
two shelters heated - includes
phone booths, seating etc...
snow melting coils in the side
walks.... sculpture...
fountains, trees, benches to
sit on...... events are now
happening -- people are all
over to ENJOY being here....

Specially
designed
incandescent
lights

now new openings
are appearing

23' carriageway

varies but
up to 45'
Sometimes one
side or the other

BUS shelter

Buses & service

special feature

thru traffic

Typical block plan

500

(500–503) Nicollet Avenue, the main street of Minneapolis, contains all its major stores but was rapidly deteriorating and beginning to lose its customers to the suburban shopping centers. After five you could have bowled a billiard ball down its sidewalks without hitting anyone. By removing all automobiles, the sidewalks could be widened and become a place for people to enjoy. All kinds of events now are possible. There are places to sit, concerts on the mall, handsome pavings, and lighting is scaled to pedestrian scale. Girl watching has started again, and even bicycles have come back into downtown. Incidentally business has improved by leaps and bounds.

501

602

603

504

505

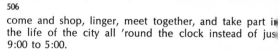

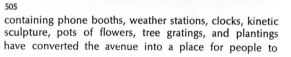

506

(504–509) The entire range of street furnishings was especially designed for the mall to convert it from a "non-descript experience" to an urbane place to be in. Pavings, bollards, light fixtures, fountains, traffic signs, bus shelters containing phone booths, weather stations, clocks, kinetic sculpture, pots of flowers, tree gratings, and plantings have converted the avenue into a place for people to come and shop, linger, meet together, and take part in the life of the city all 'round the clock instead of just 9:00 to 5:00.

507

508

509

EMBARCADERO PLAZA

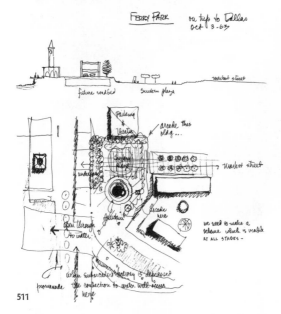

511

HALPRIN'S STATEMENT TO SCULPTORS

"This work has been conceived of as a total environment in which all the elements working together create a place for participation. The Locus is the termination of Market Street—major boulevard in the City—the Embarcadero freeway encloses the space on the east in massive and dramatic concrete and includes the movement of cars. There will be an enormous building complex to the west with terraces, platforms, shops, restaurants focusing down to the plaza. Many people.

The plaza is a theater for events to happen.

The fountain is the pivotal point in the plaza.

It has been purposely placed *off* the axis of Market Street to avoid the Renaissance quality of objects in visual static relationship and to one-point perspective.

The back wall defines the space.

It also serves as wind and sun trap.

The *sculpture* is an outgrowth of the wall and not thought of as a separate element in space. It is an environmental event in which water, light, and people are as much a part of the sculpture as are the solid forms.

It is basically made of concrete because it must be part of the environment, *not* an object within it."

510

(510) The fountain at dusk. The tower of the Ferry building is a fantasy from the past and the Embarcadero freeway a rumble from the present.

512

513

514

515

516

517

(512–517) The sculptured fountain, like a giant playground, encourages participation. People of all ages can walk through its Piranesi-like spaces, climbing up on balconies within it and walking behind the forms and water effects. Unlike the Portland cascades, the Embarcadero bears no relationship to natural forms except in the sight and sounds of the water (512–514).

At the edges of the vast brick-paved plaza grass, trees, and benches serve for picnics, noonday lunches, and just lying on the grass. The sculptural forms of the freeway have been treated as part of the composition.

PORTLAND'S PLAZAS

water sheeting over great
smooth granite blocks & at
bottom bouncing against a boulder
creating great turbulence

Sierra watercourse # 3

Halprin

The Portland fountains were designed as waterfalls echoing the natural water qualities of many of the magnificent cascades along the Columbia River and in the High Sierra. The bases for the designs were large numbers of study sketches and photographs of natural watercourses made by the author while on backpacking trips in the high country. These fountains, however, are based on an understanding of the qualities and processes of water and are not merely imitations.

520

521

522

523

524

525

526

527

PORTLAND OPEN-SPACE NETWORK

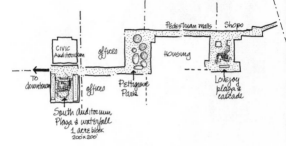

528

The sketch plan of the Portland sequence (528) shows how Lovejoy Plaza (518–527), Pettigrove Park (530–532), and Auditorium Forecourt Fountain (533–541) are connected by malls and promenades (529), forming a complete open-space network.

This eight-block-long linear sequence of open spaces, parks, plazas, fountains, waterfalls, malls, promenades, vehicular ways, and resting places acts as the living connective tissue between downtown Portland and, on through Portland Center, a large-scale redevelopment area. The urban uses that the system knits together include a cultural center, office buildings, parking structures, shops and stores, cafes and restaurants, high-rise apartment buildings, townhouses, and recreational facilities. The nodal experiences of the progression through the Portland sequence encompass vivacious Lovejoy Plaza, with its Sierra-watercourselike spumes and torrents; serene Pettigrove Park, a shady precinct of quiet green knolls for resting; and the dramatic Auditorium Forecourt Fountain, where people assemble at eleven every morning for the turning on of the waterfall. Between these experiences is a welcoming series of malls and walkways, sympathetically integrated with the street system, which provide places of respite and lead to shops, cafes, private courts, and entrances to corporate offices.

Lovejoy Plaza is situated in the residential area of Portland Center, the focal point of an all-new portion of the city. Since its opening in 1966, it has become a lure for young and old Portland residents as well as for visitors and tourists. The central fountain, with its dashing cas-

529

530

531

532

cade, splashing waterforms, and surging watercourses, was designed as a man-made evocation of the beauty and excitement of the falling, spurting, flowing, rolling cascades in the High Sierras. The pavilion above the fountain and the stepped plaza fanning out all around it form generous spaces to move in or to sit and watch the activity of the fountain and the people in it—for this fountain was designed for participation of people, not simply as a fantastic object to be looked at! And participate in it the people do: parents with babies, teenagers, young couples, mature businessmen on lunch hour, elderly people seeking the sun—all find their way to Lovejoy, and most get at least a bare foot wet. An anonymous person wrote of Lovejoy, "If I couldn't see, I'd come here just to listen and touch. It's a living creature, giving something of life to everyone."

Pettigrove Park, located midway between Lovejoy and Auditorium Forecourt, is a completely different experience. Gently rounded hillocks rise from the park, covered with inviting greenery and shaded with a canopy of trees. It is a peaceful oasis in the middle of urban Portland, a place inviting quietude, rest, and contemplation. It is not surprising that not long after its opening this was the place chosen by a young couple for the scene of their wedding ceremony.

Where Lovejoy Fountain has as its reference the water of the High Sierra, the strong concrete slabs, steles, and slanted forms of Auditorium Forecourt create a man-made reference to the cliffs and mesas of the American West. The water treatment here is quite different from Lovejoy. Where that fountain sings out from the pinnacle of the structure, Auditorium Forecourt fountain begins as a series of serene streams at the top of the block-square plaza; then, gaining in scale and intensity as it moves across the plaza, the water finally bursts from atop 80-foot-wide cliffs, to plummet 18 feet down to the pool below. Within the pool, plaza, and cliff complex are many ways for people to become involved in the spectacle of the fountain: water stairs to be ascended or descended; caves to enter behind the waterfall; pools and wading courses at both the top of the falls and down below; wide concrete stepping stones for walking across the water without getting wet; places for sitting and reclining to watch the water and the activity of other people. The lower plaza facing the falls can become an amphitheater for outdoor performances, particularly when the falls are diminished or turned off. Night lighting from below is impressive for visitors to the park or to the cultural center across the way, and the acoustics of this space have been enthusiastically acclaimed. Ada Louise Huxtable of the *New York Times*, on experiencing this moving culmination of the Portland open-space sequence, wrote that it "may be one of the most important urban spaces since the Renaissance."

533

534

535

536

537

538

539

540

541

ILLUSTRATIONS

Photographs are by Lawrence Halprin unless otherwise credited in parentheses.

1. Mirandola, Italy. Old Engraving.
2. Roman City of Turin. From Steen Eiler Rasmussen: *Towns and Buildings*.
3. Place de L'Etoile, Paris. French Government Tourist Office.
4. Times Square, New York.
5. Piazza del Duomo, Milan (Donald Ray Carter).
6. Terraces at Gap, France (Adrian Wilson).
7. Air view of an Arab town, Israel.
8. Plan of Arab town. Sketch: Lawrence Halprin.
9. Beersheba camel market, Israel. Sketch: Lawrence Halprin.
10. Arab courtyard, Acco, Israel.
11. Model of Waipio, a new town in Hawaii. Design: Livingston and Blayney; DeMars and Reay; Lawrence Halprin & Associates (Jerry Stoll).
12. Traffic model for a new town in Hawaii. Design: Livingston and Blayney.
13. Street, Cordova, Spain (Morley Baer).
14. Main Street of the old market, Nazareth, Israel.
15. Venice street scene.
16. Siena, street near Piazza del Campo.
17. Champs Elysées, Paris (Standard Oil Company, New Jersey).
18. Section of Champs Elysées. Sketch: Lawrence Halprin.
19. Proposal for Market Street, San Francisco. Design: Rockrise & Watson, Livingston and Blayney, Lawrence Halprin & Associates; Sketch: Denis R. Wilkinson of Lawrence Halprin & Associates.
20. Easter Hill Village, Richmond, California. Architects: Hardison & DeMars; Landscape Architects: Lawrence Halprin & Associates.
21. Tivoli Gardens, Copenhagen.
22. Old Orchard Shopping Center, Skokie, Illinois. Landscape Architects: Lawrence Halprin & Associates; Architects: Loebl, Schlossman & Bennett.
23. Sidewalk Cafe, Grand Canal, Venice.
24. Riva degli Schiavoni, Venice (William Lipman).
25. Pedestrian bridge, Minneapolis.
26. Capitol Towers, Sacramento, California. Landscape Architects: Lawrence Halprin & Associates; Architects: Edward L. Barnes, Wurster, Bernardi & Emmons, DeMars & Reay (Jerry Stoll).
27. Hong Kong street (Sue Yung Li).
28. Street market, Taxco, Mexico.
29. Galleria Vittorio Emanuele, Milan (Donald Ray Carter).
30. Bazaar in Shiraz, Iran (Catherine Bauer Wurster).
31. Galerie de la Reine, Brussels (Sabena Belgium World Airlines).
32. Magazin du Nord, Copenhagen (William Lipman).
33. Town Center, Stevenage, England.
34. Lijnbaan promenade, Rotterdam. Architects: Bakema & Van den Broek (William Lipman).
35. Maiden Lane, San Francisco.
36. Oakbrook Shopping Center, Oakbrook Village, Illinois. Landscape Architects: Lawrence Halprin & Associates; Architects: Loebl, Schlossman & Bennett (Ezra Stoller).
37. Old Orchard Shopping Center, Skokie, Illinois.
38. Mechanics' Plaza, San Francisco (George Knight).
39. Place du Théâtre Français, Paris.
40. Portofino, Italy (Donald Ray Carter).
41. Plaza at Capitol Towers, Sacramento. Landscape Architects: Lawrence Halprin & Associates (Morley Baer).
42. Place du Tertre, Montmartre, Paris.
43. Entrance plaza, Hebrew University, Jerusalem. Architect: S. Povsner; Landscape Architects: Lawrence Halprin & Associates (Alfred Bernheim).
44. St. Peter's Square, Rome. Bernini (Donald Ray Carter).
45. Piazza del Campo, Siena.
46. Piazza di San Marco, Venice (Richard Vignolo).
47. Union Square, San Francisco.
48. Rockefeller Plaza, New York City.
49. Rockefeller Plaza skating rink.
50. Tessin Park, Stockholm (Richard Vignolo).
51. Bedford Square, London.
52. University of California Medical School Housing, San Francisco. Landscape Architects: Lawrence Halprin & Associates; Architects: Clark & Beuttler and George Rockrise (Morley Baer).
53. Gramercy Park, New York City.
54. Canal park in Berlin.
55. Regents Park, London.
56. Central Park, New York City.
57. Princess Park, Edinburgh (Donald Ray Carter).
58. Golden Gate Park, San Francisco. Design: William Hammond Hall; Park superintendent: John McLaren (Clyde Sunderland).
59. Seine bank, Paris.
60. City Hall garden, Stockholm (John Evans).
61. Thames Embankment, London (William Lipman).
62. Fish market, Copenhagen (Standard Oil Company, New Jersey).
63. Embarcadero, San Francisco (George Knight).
64. Henry Hudson Parkway, New York City (Standard Oil Company, New Jersey).
65. East River Drive & U. N., New York City (San Francisco Dept. of Planning).
66. A Hoxton garden, London (Radio Times Hulton Picture Library).
67. Entrance to a brownstone, East 70th Street, New York City.
68. San Francisco residence. Landscape Architect: Thomas D. Church.
69. Medical Plaza, Stanford. Landscape Architects: Lawrence Halprin & Associates. Sculptor: Virginia Davidson (Morley Baer).
70. Medical Plaza, Stanford. Landscape Architects: Lawrence Halprin & Associates.
71. Medical Plaza, Stanford. Sculptor: Ray Rice.
72. Medical Plaza, Stanford. Landscape Architects: Lawrence Halprin & Associates. Architects: Wurster, Bernardi & Emmons (Morley Baer).
73,74. Communal backyards, New York City.
75,77. Greenwood Common, Berkeley, California. Architect: William Wilson Wurster; Landscape Architects: Lawrence Halprin & Associates (Morley Baer).
76. Greenwood Common, Berkeley, California. Sketch: Lawrence Halprin.
78-83. Garden, Morley Baer residence, Berkeley. Landscape Architects: Lawrence Halprin & Associates (Morley Baer).
84,85. Garden, Otto Maenchen residence, Berkeley. Architect: John Funk; Landscape Architects: Lawrence Halprin & Associates (Darrow M. Watt).
86. Garden, Peter Haas residence, San Francisco. Landscape Architects: Lawrence Halprin & Associates (Ernest Braun).
87. Garden, William Watson residence, San Francisco. Landscape Architects: Lawrence Halprin & Associates (Ernest Braun).
88. Parke-Davis, Menlo Park, California. Architect: Minoru Yamasaki; Landscape Architects: Lawrence Halprin & Associates (Roger Sturtevant).
89. Pot garden in Mexico.
90. Courtyard in Copenhagen (Adrian Wilson).
91. Balcony along Spanish Steps, Rome.
92. Backyard in N. Y. C. Designer unknown.
93. Manhattan House, New York City. Architects: Skidmore, Owings & Merrill.
94. Manhattan House, New York City. Architects: Skidmore, Owings & Merrill (Ezra Stoller).
95,96. Allotment Gardens, Berlin.
97. Market Street, San Francisco (George Rockrise).
98. Sailor on Market Street, San Francisco (Jerry Stoll).
99. Proposal for Market Street, San Francisco. Design: Lawrence Halprin & Associates, Livingston and Blayney, Rockrise & Watson; Sketch: Denis R. Wilkinson of Lawrence Halprin & Associates.
100. Student Union, University of California, Berkeley. Architects: DeMars & Reay; Landscape Architects: Lawrence Halprin & Associates (Morley Baer).
101. U. S. Science Pavilion, Seattle World's Fair. Architects: Minoru Yamasaki & Associates; Landscape Architects: Lawrence Halprin & Associates (Glenn Christiansen).
102. Light pattern, San Francisco at night (Donald Ray Carter).
103,104. Tivoli Gardens, Copenhagen.
105. Piccadilly Circus, London (Donald Ray Carter).
106. Piccadilly Circus at night (Donald Ray Carter).
107. Piazza del Duomo, Milan, at night.
108. Duomo, Milan, early morning.
109. Duomo, Milan, afternoon.
110. Piazzetta di San Marco, Venice (William Lipman).
111. Light standard, Florence.
112. Light standard, Amalienborg Plads, Copenhagen (Donald Ray Carter).
113. Light standard, Old Orchard Shopping Center, Skokie, Illinois. Designers: Lawrence Halprin & Associates.
114. Light standard, Davis, California. Design: Lawrence Halprin & Associates.
115. Highway light standard (William Lipman).
116. Light standard, Spokane, Washington. Design: Bruce Walker.
117. Light standard, Sacramento, California. Design: Lawrence Halprin & Associates (Morley Baer).
118. Parque Maria Luisa, Sevilla, Spain (Morley Baer).
119. Bench dimensions. Sketch: Lawrence Halprin.
120. Foothill Square Shopping Center, Oakland, California. Bench design: Lawrence Halprin & Associates.
121. Double bench, Florence (Donald Ray Carter).
122. Tile bench, Mexico City.
123. Mosaic bench, Boboli Gardens, Florence.
124. Wrought iron bench, Mexico (John Evans).
125. Bench, Crawley, England (William Lipman).
126. Bench, Coventry, England (William Lipman).
127. Bench, Paris.
128. Lucerne, Switzerland (Donald Ray Carter).
129. U. S. Science Pavilion, Seattle World's Fair. Architects: Minoru Yamasaki & Associates.
130. Washington Water Power Company, Spokane. Design: Lawrence Halprin & Associates.
131. University of California, at Davis. Design: Lawrence Halprin & Associates.

INDEX